FULL STACK WEB DEVELOPMENT GUIDE

Everything HTML 5, CSS 3, Bootstrap 4, JavaScript, jQuery, GIT, GITHUB, and Version Control for Modern Web Development

---

SAMMIE SMITH

TABLE OF CONTENT

CHAPTER ONE

INTRODUCTION

The rise of the electronic computer, the World Wide Web, and the Internet are the ultimate inventions of this age or century, and we are fortunate to be witnesses of these inventions, working on the peak of the trend that the influence of these inventions is having on the human race.

Developers of different levels have typically worked in technological companies, or within technological departments of different organizations, but as the older developers are now getting old because of a lack of upskilling and are now retiring, the modern generation is finding expression and gaining employment in many different areas in the tech world.

Also, web development is one of the skills that is highly sought after in the world today. It's a skill that has continued to experience high take-home currencies. Employment of web developers and digital designers has been projected to grow 13 percent from 2020, to 2030. Web development, over the past years, had been reduced to building just websites. But web development truly goes beyond just building websites, to building apps, games, virtual assistance, and other resources that run on the web. I would recommend that in choosing a career in one of the good number Tech skills you must have seen or read about, Web Development is a wonderful start. All of these factors have given rise to the "full stack" development.

This publication series is focused on the modern Front-end development technologies and the next series shall discuss the Back-end technology tools alongside the Database technology tools and every other technology involved in the modern-day full-stack development tools.

What is Full Stack Web Development?

Full Stack web development involves the activities of both front-end and back-end web development. Full Stack developers are knowledgeable in every level and layer of how the web works. They are also seen as Jack of all trades, understanding every system and component that make up the web. They can build solutions to every problem on the web. It requires the indebt knowledge of the different scripting languages like HTML, CSS, and JavaScript, which makes the web looks more attractive. It also requires in-depth knowledge of high-level programming languages such as Java, Python, PHP, C++, C#, Visual Basic, and so on to code a server side. Apart from these, you also require experience in working with JavaScript frameworks like NodeJS, libraries, JQuery, and so on, APIs design, and database application tools inclusive.

Layers of Full Stack Development

Full Stack Web Development speaks of the development of both the front end and back end of web applications or web applications. The Full Stack web development process consists of three layers, which include:

- **The presentation layer**: This consists of the front end of the application. This means the HTML, CSS, and JavaScript that users interact with. Other application types are mobile applications, desktop applications, and voice interfaces. Nevertheless, sticking with strictly Web applications, is where you'll come across the Web page that the client works with.
- **The logic layer**: This consists of the back end of the application. It should safely retrieve and place data requested or given from the consuming client and pass it along to the data layer. This often involves more complicated tasks like authentication, authorization, API design, or creating the logic to implement business logic.
- **The database layer**: The database layer, which is also recognized as the data tier, stores all the information connected to user profiles and transactions. Principally, it consists of any data that needs to persist in being stored in the data tier.

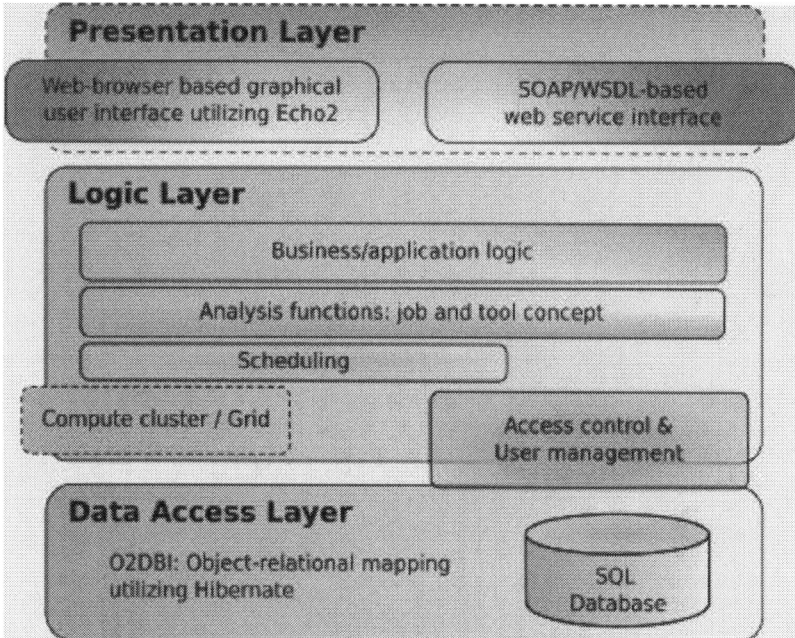

Who is a Full Stack Web Developer?

A Full Stack Web Developer is a developer who can work on both ends of the web development process, i.e., front end and back end. They are capable of performing the following tasks:

- Writing optimized front-end code in HTML, CSS, JavaScript, and Java.
- In-depth understanding of the system's infrastructure such as how hardware and OS work.
- Security and Networking in web development.
- Designing APIs and writing backend code in Python, Java, and PHP.
- Client interactions and Project Management Skills.
- Creating and querying databases.

So, it can be said that a full-stack web developer can build strategies for every part of the web development process. They can get in-depth knowledge of the various stacks through years of experience in the technical field and the zeal to learn new technologies in the market.

It is quite difficult to gather and possess these skills and that is the reason why full-stack web developers are hugely in-demand in the industry.

Why are full-stack web developers in high demand at present?

The demand for full stack developers is high as likened to the developers who are only specialized in one layer of a technology stack. The main reason that has led to the great demand for full-stack web development specialists is the persistent pace of technologies. Also, technologies being used today are entirely different as it was used to be ten years back.

Developers can keep up with the rapid changes in technology since full-stack development requires a wide variety of abilities. They can construct the full working prototype on their own because they are familiar with every layer of the technology stack.

Organizations that need to create a Minimum Feasible Product as quickly as possible while considering the needs of the client will benefit from the capacity of full stack developers to operate across various stacks.

Every full stack developer should be able to work on every layer of the application and produce finished products in the shortest amount of time. The market need for full-stack web developers has grown as a result of their contribution to many stages of the development life cycle. You must understand all the skills you require if you want to work as a full-stack developer.

How to become a Full Stack Web Developer?

Every full-stack developer should have practical knowledge and capabilities for all areas which involve the building of software applications. The screenshot below shows the full-stack development tools that every potential full-stack developer or individual desiring to be a full-stack developer should learn.

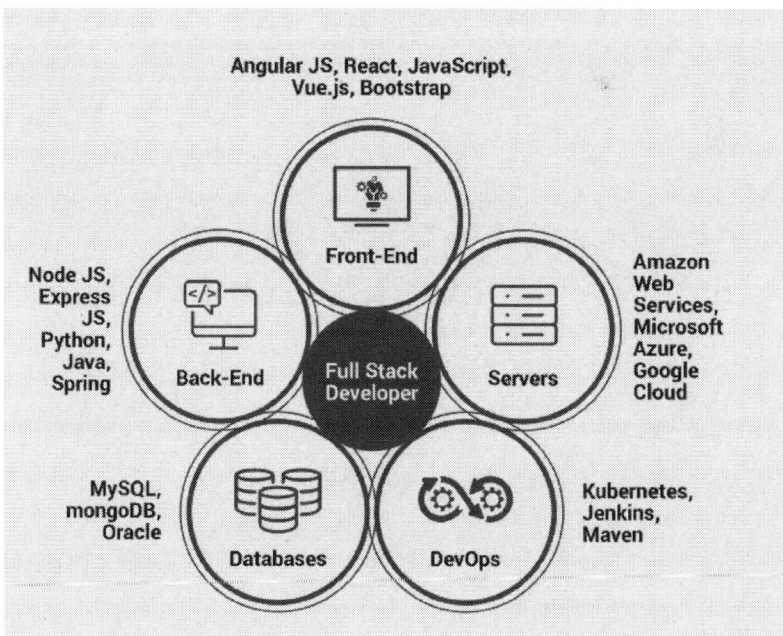

Every developer must have in-depth knowledge of the following:

- **Programming Languages:** Every developer needs to be an expert in multiple programming languages like Java, C#, PHP, Python, and many more. However most of the core business developments are written in these languages, therefore, every full stack developer needs to master the syntax of languages and be conversant with how to design, structure, and test projects based on those programming languages.

- Knowledge of development frameworks and third-party libraries: A full-stack web developer should have a good understanding of various web development frameworks that support rapid application development. They should know which web development framework can be suitable for the type of application they want to build. The programming languages cited above are accompanied by development frameworks and third-party libraries like Java Spring, Angular, Django, PHP, and so on.

- **Front-end Technology**: Front-end technologies play a fundamental role in the development of every application. In addition to the user interface and product structures, the user experience is also one of the paramount benchmarks to test the product's accomplishment. Hence, a full-stack web developer has to be professional in some of the necessary front-end technologies like HTML5, JavaScript, TypeScript,

7

CSS, JS Frameworks, DOM Sass, HTTP, and BootStrap.

- **Back-end Technology**: Once you get a decent understanding of front-end tools like JavaScript, CSS, HTML, and others, you have to move on to the back-end technologies to handle tasks such as database management, user authentication, and application logic. You may come across a good number of backend technologies, but you will have to discover one that meets the conditions of the project you are working on. Node.js, Python, Java, PHP, and Ruby are some of the trending backend technologies which you can learn to implement across numerous applications.

- **Database Management**: Although, in becoming a full stack web developer, you would also have to save the data of the software application somewhere and use it at later stages. As a full-stack web developer, you also need to have a comprehensive understanding of the technologies related to storage and databases. You must understand the following:

1. The basics of relational data. For instance, how to connect an application with SQL and how to run queries.

2. You should also learn about NoSQL databases, such as MongoDB.

3. Know how to connect a database with backend technology. For instance, Java+SQL.

8

4. Study about the benefits of in-memory data stores like Memcached and Redis.

5. Know how to use web storage for storing sessions, cached data, and cookies in the browser.

6. Know about scaling databases, ORM, and ACID.

You must make sure you have a super understanding of the above database concepts to become a professional in full-stack web development.

- **Web application architecture**: When you are done learning about front-end and back-end programming tools and databases, a developer needs to know the architecture of a web application. If you have to develop a complex and enormous web application, you should know how to organize your code, how to keep files structured, how to arrange the data in databases, where to host the media files, and where to perform computational jobs. To understand how to handle large and complicated applications, you should:

1. Learn about the common platforms as a service, like AWS and Heroku. AWS makes available lots of services and products to assist with video processing, storage, and load matching. On the other hand, Heroku permits you to upload the code and application proficiently running with server maintenance.

2. Learn about performance optimization for present browsers and web applications.

3. Also, consider the codebases of prevalent projects on GitHub to learn how to manage the structural design of web applications.

- **HTTP and REST**: HTTP is known to be a stateless application protocol that permits client applications to interrelate with servers. A full-stack developer ought to understand how HTTP requests are managed at the backend of the application.

The following are some of the topics you should learn to know more about HTML or REST

- Study HTTP/2 and SPDY.
- Understand REST and how it is related to HTTP.
- Understand SSL Certificates.
- Learn how to use Chrome DevTools.
- Understand Web Sockets, Service Workers and Web Workers.

Basic Data Structures and Algorithms

In this day and age, a lot of developers believe that learning algorithms like matrix manipulation, tree traversal, or sorting are not necessary for web development. Nevertheless, big companies hire full-stack developers who have a strong computer science background.

In becoming a reputable full-stack web developer, you must have a good understanding of the following:

1. Understand Hash tables and what ways they are applied in a real application.
2. Know how graphs and trees can be beneficial and applied in real time.
3. Understand the difference between linked lists and arrays.
4. Understand the difference between queues and stacks.
- **Decentralized Technology:** With the capacity to bring trust, and transparency to the core commercial processes, decentralized technology is attaining a lot of financial traction nowadays. To stay ahead of the technology arc, you ought also to understand the concepts of decentralized, various categories of blockchain technology platforms, and how they work at the backend development.

You should also make sure you have a good understanding of the following concepts:

1. Understand Distributed Ledger Technology.
2. Know the different types of consensus algorithms.
3. Understand blockchain technologies and how they work.
4. How to build an application using different blockchain platforms.
5. Understand the difference between various blockchain platforms.

Becoming a full-stack web developer is not a stress-free task, because you need to learn multiple technology stacks if you must stand out.

Concepts of the Web every Developer needs to know

WEB: The web is also known as Word Wide Web (WWW) or W3, it's an interconnected system of public webpages usually known as servers. The WWW is a web technology that Links web resources together over the internet. The Web is not the same as the Internet, but the Web is one of many applications built on top of the Internet because the internet housed the Web.

URL: Uniform Resource Locator (URL) also known as Web address is a reference to a web resource that specifies its location on a computer network and a gateway for retrieving it. A typical example of a URL is https://www.google.com. Https represent the Transfer Control Protocol, while Google.com is the URL for Google.

HTTPS: Hypertext Transfer Protocol Secured is a secured protocol that governs the transfer of Web resources. While Hypertext Transfer Protocol is a none secured protocol that governs the transfer of Web resources. You can identify between this two when surfing the internet. Secured protocol usually puts a visible padlock before the address bar of the Web browser while none secured does not.

WEBSITE: A website is said to be a collection of related web pages with common web resources and share the same domain name. A web page may consist of text, images, audio, video animations, and other related resources. These resources could be static or dynamic. There are primarily two (2) types of websites; Static and Dynamic Websites.

DOMAIN NAME: Domain is simply your website address. It is a unique name that identifies resources stored on a website. It's a unique name that houses your website. Because of the above definition, two websites cannot have the same name, but a website can have a primary domain and a sub-domain. The primary domain is said to be the main domain name of a website. For instance, facebook.com, google.com, etc. While the sub-domain is a secondary domain to the primary domain. For instance app.facebook.com, app.google.com, etc.

HOSTING: Hosting serves as the land upon which your website is built. Web hosting servers are the space where your website is built and stored which is accessible on the web.

SERVER: A server is a software or hardware device that accepts and responds to requests made over a network. The device that makes the request, and receives a response from the server, is called a client. On the Internet, the term "server" commonly refers to the computer system that receives requests for a web file and sends those files to the client. Servers manage network resources. For example, a user may set up a server to control access to a network, send/receive an e-mail, manage print jobs, or host a website. They are also proficient at performing intense calculations. Some servers are committed to a specific task, often referred to as dedicated. However, many servers today are shared servers that take on the responsibility of e-mail, DNS, FTP, and even multiple websites in the case of a web server.

Understanding the types of Web

1. **Web 1.0**: Web 1.0, also called the Static Web, was the first available and most reliable internet in the 1990s notwithstanding the fact it gives access to limited information with little to no user interaction. Back in the day, creating user pages or even remarking on articles wasn't possible since it was not built with such a feature.

   Web 1.0 didn't have algorithms to sift internet pages and bring them together in a dynamic way, which made it extremely hard for users to find relevant information. Simply put, it was like a one-way highway with a narrow footpath where content creation was done by a select few algorithms and information came mostly from directories where they are stored.

2. **Web 2.0**: Web 2.0, also known as Social Web, or Web 2.0, made the internet a lot more interactive. Here, messages can be exchanged on a real-time basis. The advancements in web technologies like JavaScript, HTML5, CSS3, etc. It enabled startups to build interactive web platforms such as YouTube, Facebook, Wikipedia, and lots more. This paved the way for both social networks and user-generated content production to flourish since businessmen and women can run business adverts on those platforms, thereby promoting their products and services. Data can now

be distributed and shared between various platforms and applications.

3. **Web 3.0**: Web 3.0 is the third generation of the internet where websites and applications will be able to process information in a smart human-like way through technologies like Big Data, machine learning (ML), decentralized ledger technology (DLT), etc. Web 3.0 was originally called the Semantic Web by World Wide Web inventor Tim Berners-Lee, and was aimed at being a more autonomous, intelligent, and open internet. The Web 3.0 definition can be expanded as follows: data will be interconnected in a decentralized way, which would be a huge leap forward to our current generation of the internet unlike (Web 2.0), where data is mostly stored in centralized repositories or systems. The two functions of Web 3.0 is the semantic web and artificial intelligence (AI). Web 3.0 is the succeeding stage of the web evolution that would make the internet more intellectual or process information with near-human-like brainpower through the power of AI systems that can run smart programs to assist users.

Tim Berners-Lee had said that the Semantic Web is meant to "automatically" interface with people, systems, and home devices without the need for a middleman. As such, content creation and decision-making processes will include both humans and machines. This would allow the intelligent creation and distribution of highly-tailored content straight to every internet end user.

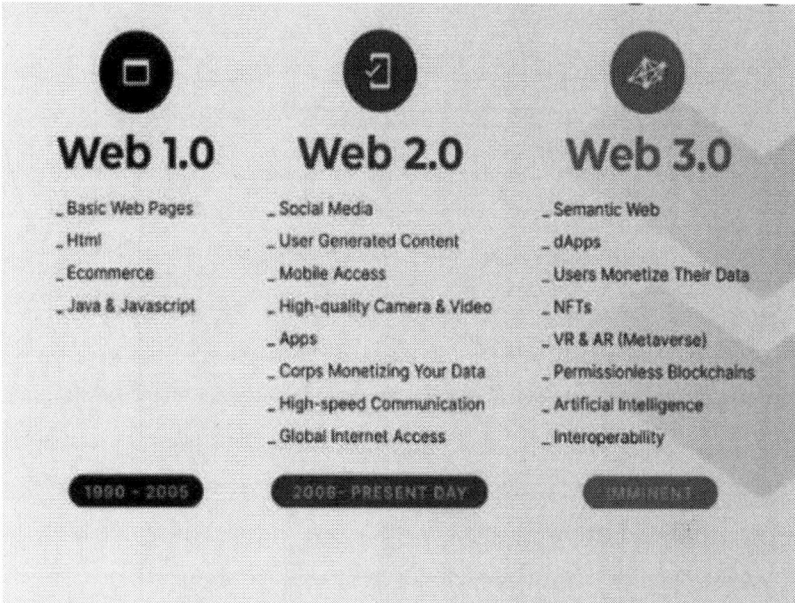

Web 1.0	Web 2.0	Web 3.0
_ Basic Web Pages	_ Social Media	_ Semantic Web
_ Html	_ User Generated Content	_ dApps
_ Ecommerce	_ Mobile Access	_ Users Monetize Their Data
_ Java & Javascript	_ High-quality Camera & Video	_ NFTs
	_ Apps	_ VR & AR (Metaverse)
	_ Corps Monetizing Your Data	_ Permissionless Blockchains
	_ High-speed Communication	_ Artificial Intelligence
	_ Global Internet Access	_ Interoperability
1990 - 2005	2006 - PRESENT DAY	IMMINENT

Understanding Web Development

Web development is the building and maintenance of websites; the process involved in building solutions to problems or programs that runs on the web. It's knowing the concepts and ways of building solutions to programs. These programs cut across the building and maintenance of apps, games, and other resources that run on the web.

A Web Designer and a Web Developer

A Web Designer: A web designer is said to be a graphic artist who is responsible for designing the layout that is, the user interfaces, and the visual look of a website. A web designer must possess and sustain a level of creativity in graphics manipulations, and have knowledge of WordPress, HTML, and CSS, with other technical skills.

16

A Web Developer: A web developer is tasked with the responsibility of translating the results of a web designer into a functional website, using coding languages such as HTML, CCS, JavaScript, Node Js, MongoDB, React, Vue Js, Angular, PHP, Python, and other programming languages. They are up to date in knowing the concepts it takes to build and maintain programs that run on the web. A web developer is someone who builds and maintains the core structure of a website. They are often used interchangeably with Web Engineers. But a Web Engineer is a senior brother to a web developer. Because they understood the functionalities of software development stages and can work at every development stage. Their responsibility is to give instructions to web developers.

Types of Web Developers

There are three major types of web developers, and they are as follows.

1. **Frontend**: A frontend developer is saddled with the responsibility of building layouts or the user interface of a website. They are the good guys that the users relate with, their impact is felt by the users because they have a direct relationship with them. Frontend developers combine their vast knowledge of HTML, CSS, JavaScript, and other languages, as well as Content Management systems (CMS) such as WordPress, to create user interfaces or layouts of a website.

Frontend development, also known as client-side development, largely involves coding and programming the visual elements of a website that users will see.

2. **Backend**: Backend developers are responsible for database structure, functionality, and server using advanced programming languages such as PHP, C#, Java, Ruby, and SQL, as well as Node JS, Angular JS, React, and other server-side frameworks. Back-end development, also known as server-side development, mainly encompasses the aspects of the website happening 'behind the scenes, which visitors don't see from the front end.

3. **Full-Stack**: Full-stack developers combined the functions of both the front end and the back end of a website. They have a solid understanding of how these parts work and function together. In addition to coding web pages using CSS, HTML, and JavaScript, full-stack developers also set up and configure servers, code Application Programming Interfaces (APIs), query databases, and some other functions.

(NB: The frontend, backend, and Full Stack developers are mostly called coders. This is because they are responsible for building codes for programs, or building solutions to programs that run on the web).

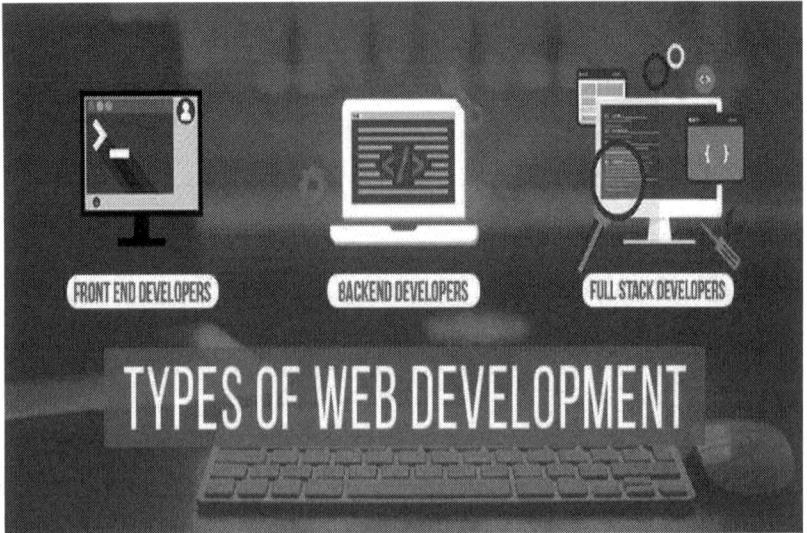

FRONT END DEVELOPERS   BACKEND DEVELOPERS   FULL STACK DEVELOPERS

TYPES OF WEB DEVELOPMENT

Understanding Web Technology Stacks

A tech stack is defined as the set of software tools or technologies an individual or organization uses to build a web or mobile application. It is a combination of different programming languages, mark-up languages, style sheets, frameworks, libraries, patterns, servers, UI/UX (User Interface/User Experience) solutions, software, and tools used by web developers. A technology stack, also known as a software stack or development stack is categorically divided into two: client-side (frontend) and server-side (backend). Backend tools or technologies include web frameworks, programming languages, servers, and operating systems, while frontend tools or technologies include HTML, CSS, JavaScript, and UI frameworks and libraries. It refers to the software tools or technologies developers specialize in and combine to develop new pieces of software. They are mainly; MongoDB, NodeJS, ExpressJS, AngularJS, VueJS, React, MySQL, PostgreSQL, etc.

Front-End, Client-Side Technology Stack

Every web application has two different sides. One is accessible to the client and is accountable for the UI, while the other is accountable for the client's experience. The side which is visible to the client and exploited by him/her to communicate with the application constitutes the front end. The front-end technology stack primarily consists of HTML, CSS, Java, and so forth.

- **HTML**: It is a Markup Language utilized for rendering the creation of data introduced on a page. Also, it employs the most recent rendition of HTML, HTML5 which has new mechanisms and what it takes for making web applications all the more effective and viably. The essential benefit that HTML5 has is, its sound and video support, which was omitted from past versions of HTML.
- **CSS**: It is a template language that represents the look, position, and design of a document written in HTML. CSS is used for explaining text and inserting labels in styled electronic documents.
- **JavaScript**: It is the third principal technology for building the front end of a web application. It is regularly utilized for making dynamic and intuitive site pages. Besides, it also empowers basic and complex web animations, which significantly add to a positive client experience. JavaScript helps to make easy-to-

understand applications in addition to this subject. You can check some collections of admin templates based on HTML, CSS, and JS here at React bootstrap admin template free, Bootstrap 5 admin template GitHub, and Bootstrap Admin Templates.

Back-End, Server-Side Technology Stack

The working of the application is dependent on the client association primarily with the back end or server side. It isn't available to the client, and the technology that is answerable for creating that association is known as the back-end technology stack. Programming languages, structures, libraries, servers, data set administration frameworks, etc., are vital parts of back-end tech stacks. It refers to the technologies they major in and uses together to create new pieces of software. The backend technology stack mainly consists of the following programming tools:

NodeJS, MongoDB, ExpressJS, Angular, React, Vue, Postgr eSQL, MySQL, Apache, etc.

The backend stack incorporates the following components:

1. **Programming languages**: This makes reasoning for applications and sites easy. It provides the code interface and the web data set. A few representations are JavaScript, PHP, and Python.
2. **Frameworks**: This offers help for applications reliant on a single programming language. Django, Laravel, and Ruby on Rails are many of the well-known technologies in this regard.

3. **Web Servers**: You need backend servers to oversee customer demands. Apache, Nginx, and Microsoft's Internet Information Server (IIS) are extraordinary instances of web servers.

CHAPTER TWO

WEB DEVELOPMENT FUNDAMENTALS

Understand how websites work and how HTML, CSS, and JavaScript contribute

A website is normally the assemblage of web pages. These web pages may consist of texts, images, audio, videos, and other elements that are linked together to form a large structured document. A website could be made up of a single page or thousands of pages assembled. Each page will have its text, images, and other elements. All web pages and their elements are then retained in a folder and stored on your web host server. Each web page is written in codes and these codes define the layout, format, and content on the page. The most common website coding technologies are HTML, CSS, and JavaScript.

HTML, CSS, and JavaScript work together to form the foundation of your website, which is the front-end design of a website. HTML, CSS, and JavaScript are considered to be the backbone of the web. These three design tools are for front-end web development and are responsible for what you can see and relate to on a website. They are referred to as client-side technologies as they run in the browser (Microsoft Edge, Google Chrome, Firefox, etc.) of your computer. The browser does the translation of these design tools and the result of this translation is the visual web page.

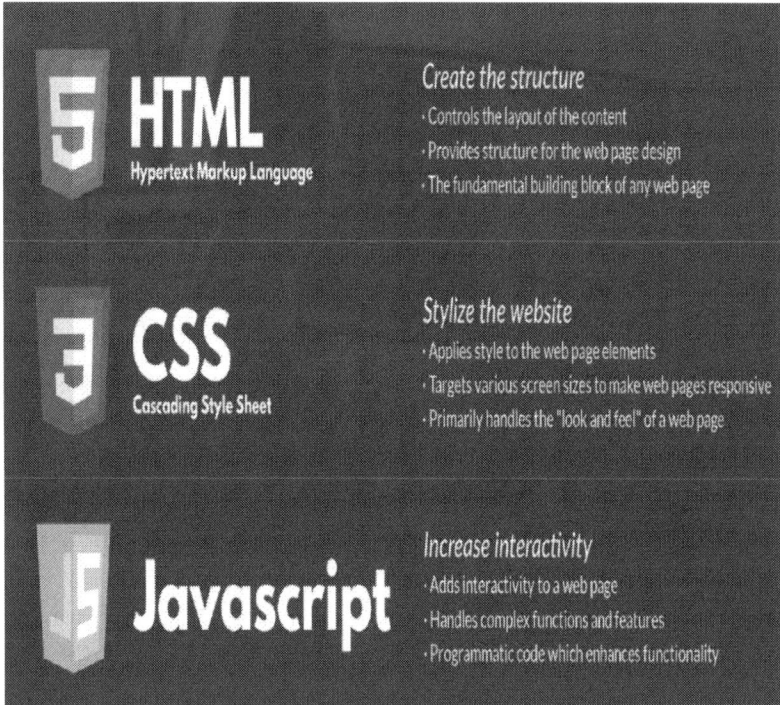

HTML
Hypertext Markup Language

Create the structure
· Controls the layout of the content
· Provides structure for the web page design
· The fundamental building block of any web page

CSS
Cascading Style Sheet

Stylize the website
· Applies style to the web page elements
· Targets various screen sizes to make web pages responsive
· Primarily handles the "look and feel" of a web page

Javascript

Increase interactivity
· Adds interactivity to a web page
· Handles complex functions and features
· Programmatic code which enhances functionality

Understand how the internet works

The Internet is defined as a network of networks. It works by using a technology called packet switching, which relies on standardized networking protocols that all computers can interpret. The internet is a worldwide computer network that transfers a diversity of data and media through interconnected devices. It works by using a packet routing network that follows Internet Protocol (IP) and Transfer Control Protocol (TCP). TCP and IP work together to make sure that data transmission through the internet is steady and reliable, no matter the device you're using or where you're using it. As soon as data is transmitted over the internet, it's distributed in messages and packets. Data sent through the

24

internet is termed a message, but before messages get sent, they're fragmented into the smallest form called packets.

These messages and packets journey from one source to another using Internet Protocol (IP) and Transfer Control Protocol (TCP). Internet Protocol is a system of guidelines that directs how information is sent from one computer to another computer through an internet connection. Using a numerical IP Address, the IP system accepts additional instructions on how the data is to be transferred. The Transfer Control Protocol (TCP) works together with IP to guarantee the transfer of data process is trustworthy and reliable. This supports making sure that no packets are lost, packets are reconvened in a proper sequence, and there's no postponement adversely affecting the data quality.

Start coding with HTML, CSS, and JavaScript

The most important part of this lesson is to start learning how to code with HTML, CSS, and JavaScript. Before you can do this, you will have to get one of the editor technology tools to actualize this. You could use Atom editor, Visual Studio Code editor, or Sublime Text 3. It's also important to note that HTML and CSS are not programming languages. HTML is a markup language while CSS is a styling language. JavaScript, however, is a programming language. Hence, they are all web languages for building a specific part of a website.

Learn and understand Git, GitHub, and Version Control

Have you been wondering how Git and GitHub work? Don't worry, you are not alone in that confusion. Git and GitHub can be confusing sometimes, but when you follow them gently you will be able to grasp the technology behind them.

When you hear of these two techniques, it may be tempting to believe Git and GitHub are the same things. But in actuality, they are not. Certainly, it is workable to use Git without GitHub! And eventually, these two exist with dissimilar intentions.

What is GitHub?

GitHub is a website and cloud-based technology that helps developers store and manage their code, as well as keep track and control modifications to their code. To understand exactly what GitHub is, you need to understand Version control and Git principles.

Understanding Git Technology

Git is a Distributed Version Control System (DVCS) used to preserve different versions of a file or set of files so that any of the saved versions are retrievable at will. Git also makes it stress-free to record and compare, unlike file versions. This means that the details about what is to be changed, who does the change, or who instigated an issue are reviewable anytime.

What does distributed mean?

The term **distributed** means that each time you instruct Git to distribute or share a project's directory with the individual in view, Git does not only share the up-to-date file version. Instead, it distributes every version it has documented for that project. This distributed system is a sharp difference from other version control systems. They only distribute whatever single version a user has openly checked out from the principal or local database. Consequently, distributing means distributing all files and not just the selected few versions of a project's files that Git has documented.

Understanding files states in Git

Git has three primary states or conditions in which a file can be, and they are explained below.

1. **Modified state**: A file in the modified state is a revised file but uncommitted is an unrecorded file. In other words, files in the modified state are files you have revised but have not authorized Git to monitor.

2. **Staged state**: Files in the staged state are modified files that have been carefully selected in their current state or version and are being organized to be saved or committed into the .git storehouse or repository during the next commit caption. Once a file gets staged, it indicates that you have clearly instructed Git to monitor that file's version.

3. **Committed state**: Files in the committed state are files that are successfully warehoused into the .git repository. Hence, a committed file is a file in

which you have recorded its staged version into the Git directory or folder.

(NB: The state of a file defines the location where Git will place it).

Follow the steps below to host or share a Git repository on GitHub.

1. Signup for a GitHub account.

2. Create a remote repository in GitHub.

3. Connect the project's Git directory to the remote repository.

4. Confirm the connection.

5. Push a local Git repo to the remote repo.

(NB: When you have successfully connected your local directory to the remote repository, you can then begin to push, that is, upload your local project upstream, and whenever you are ready to share your project elsewhere, on any remote repo, you can simply authorize Git to push all your commits, branches, and files in your local .git directory to the remote repository. The code syntax used to upload or push a local Git directory to a remote repository is: git push -u remoteName branchName).

6. Confirm the upload by going back to your GitHub repository page to confirm that Git has successfully pushed your local Git directory to the remote repository as instructed.

(NB: You may need to refresh the remote repository's page for the changes to reflect).

What is Version Control?

A Version Control System (VCS) refers to the technique used to save a file's versions for future use. Version control is a technology that helps developers track and manage modifications to a software project's code. As a project grows, version control becomes indispensable. With branching, a developer can duplicate part of the source code called the repository. After this, the developer can then safely make modifications to that part of the code without changing the rest of the project.

At that time, the developer gets his or her part of the code working appropriately, he or she can merge that code back into the main source code to make it official. All of these changes are then tracked and can be reverted if need be.

Unthinkingly, several people already version control their project's work by retitling different versions of the same file in different ways like storeScript.js, storeScript_v2.js, storeScript_v3.js, store Script_final.js, storeScript_definite_final.js, etc. But this approach is prone to error and unproductive for team projects. Similarly, tracking what is being changed, who changed it, and why it was changed is a boring endeavor with this old-style approach. This lightens the significance of a dependable and collaborative version control system like Git.

However, to get the best of Git, it is essential to understand how Git handles your files.

Finally, Git and GitHub are two dissimilar entities that assist you to manage and host files. In other words, Git serves to control file versions while GitHub is a platform for hosting Git repositories.

Learn the Unix command line to become a power user and write bash commands

A Unix shell is a command-line translator or shell that offers a command-line user interface for Unix-like operating systems. Unix and Unix-based Operating Systems such as macOS and Linux have always included their main Command Line Interface (CLI) such as a terminal window. While for most of its existence, Microsoft drives people to disregard their command prompt options and to strictly work within the graphical user interface, starting with Windows 7, Microsoft has included their PowerShell command-line shell and scripting language. The shell is both a collaborative command language and a scripting language and is used by the operating system to manage the execution of the programs using shell scripts. The Unix (Ultrix) operating system is case-sensitive. All commands must be typed in lower-case letters unless noted otherwise. Unix command can help in achieving the following task.

- Can be used in Displaying a Directory.

- Displaying and Concatenating (Combining) Files.

- Copying Files.

- Deleting Files.

- Renaming Files.

- Printing from Unix, etc.

Understanding the concept of Bash Command

Bash is a Unix shell and command language designed by Brian Fox for the GNU Project as an unrestricted software substitute for the Bourne shell. First relinquish in 1989, it has been used as the default login shell for most Linux distributions. Bash was one of the first programs Linus Torvalds ported to Linux, alongside GCC. The Bash command is located at /usr/bin/which. Most of the command tools are located under the /usr/bin directory. Here, bash is consulting PATH for the places to search for the executable(s) of a command.

What is Bash (Bourne Again Shell)?

Bash (Bourne Again Shell) is the open and improved version of the Bourne shell distributed with Linux and GNU operating systems. Bash is similar to the original, but has added several other features such as command-line editing.

It was created to improve on the earlier Bourne shell (named sh), Bash includes features from the Korn shell and the C shell. Bash is envisioned to fit into the shell standard specified as part of IEEE POSIX. A command language script written for the Bourne shell should also run in the bash shell.

What is a shell?

A shell is a program that provides entrance to an operating system's modules. The shell provides users or other programs a passage to get inside the entire system; the shell defines the margin between inside and outside.

There are two types of operating system shells, which are:

1. Command-line interface (CLI) shells, like bash, provide users a concise and efficient mode of interrelating with the Operating System, without demanding the overhead of a graphic user interface.
2. Graphical user interface (GUI) shells, such as Windows and macOS, are well thought-out and easier for starters to use, but usually, also provide programs that imitate a CLI-based shell for system administrators or other power users who prefer to interact at a command prompt.

Bash is the most commonly used CLI shell for Unix-based OSes, including Linux.

What is bash used for?

Bash, like other CLIs, is used for any computer application that requires accuracy when dealing with files and data, specifically where large numbers of files or large amounts of data need to be searched, sorted, manipulated, or processed in any way. Bash is commonly used interactively, but it can also be used to write shell scripts. Almost any computer task can be automated using a Bash script. Bash scripts can be run on-demand or scheduled to run occasionally.

How does bash work?

At first sight, bash appears to be a simple command/response system, where users input commands and bash returns the results after those commands are executed. However, bash is also a programming platform, and users are allowed to write programs that take in input and produce output using shell commands in shell scripts.

One of the most basic bash commands, ls, does one thing: list directory contents. By itself, this command lists only the names of files and subdirectories in the present working directory.

Some frequently used parameters used with the ls command are shown in the screenshot below:

ls command-line arguments (parameters)	Purpose
-l	Use a longer, more detailed, listing format to include file permissions, file owner, group, size, and date/time of creation.
-a	List all files and subdirectories, even those that are ordinarily intended to be hidden.
-s	Display the size of each file.
-h	Display file and subdirectory sizes in a human-readable format using K, M, G, and so on to indicate kilobytes, megabytes, and gigabytes.
-R	Recursive listing of all files and subdirectories under the current working directory.

When you use all the above parameters together, these parameters give the user a much clearer sense of what files and subdirectories are in a directory, when they have last been changed and who changed them.

See the screenshot below showing the directories and subdirectories and when they were last changed.

```
peterloshin@penguin /$ ls
bin  boot  dev  etc  home  lib  lib64  media  mnt  opt  proc  root  run  sbin  srv  sys  ▓  usr  var
peterloshin@penguin /$ ls -lash
total 0
0 drwxrwxrwx  1 root    root     132 Nov 30 11:08 █
0 drwxrwxrwx  1 root    root     132 Nov 30 11:08 █
0 drwxr-xr-x  1 root    root    1.5K Aug 31 00:02 bin
0 drwxr-xr-x  1 root    root       0 Jun 13 06:30 boot
0 drwxr-xr-x 12 root    root     660 Nov 30 09:53 dev
0 drwxr-xr-x  1 root    root    2.2K Nov 30 09:58 etc
0 drwxr-xr-x  1 root    root      22 Nov 30 09:52 home
0 drwxr-xr-x  1 root    root     126 Aug 31 00:02 lib
0 drwxr-xr-x  1 root    root      40 Aug 30 14:52 lib64
0 drwxr-xr-x  1 root    root       0 Aug 30 14:52 media
0 drwxr-xr-x  1 root    root      32 Nov 30 09:52 mnt
0 drwxr-xr-x  1 root    root      12 Nov 30 09:52 opt
0 dr-xr-xr-x 187 nobody nogroup    0 Nov 30 09:52 proc
0 drwx------  1 root    root      30 Aug 30 14:52 root
0 drwxr-xr-x 13 root    root     400 Nov 30 11:19 run
0 drwxr-xr-x  1 root    root    1.7K Aug 31 00:02 sbin
0 drwxr-xr-x  1 root    root       0 Aug 30 14:52 srv
0 dr-xr-xr-x 12 nobody nogroup    0 Nov 30 09:52 sys
0 drwxrwxrwt  1 root    root      94 Nov 30 11:20 █
0 drwxr-xr-x  1 root    root      80 Aug 31 00:03 usr
0 drwxr-xr-x  1 root    root      90 Aug 30 14:52 var
peterloshin@penguin /$ ls -lash /home
total 0
0 drwxr-xr-x 1 root           root          22 Nov 30 09:52 .
0 drwxrwxrwx 1 root           root         132 Nov 30 11:08 █
0 drwxr-xr-x 1 peterloshin peterloshin 192 Nov 30 11:08 peterloshin
peterloshin@penguin /$ ls -lashR /home | grep "filename.txt"
4.0K -rw-r--r-- 1 peterloshin peterloshin  15 Nov 30 11:07 filename.txt
peterloshin@penguin /$ █
```

Types of bash commands include:

- **Simple commands**: They are usually run by themselves or with parameters and variables. For instance, the ls command takes parameters as well as variables relating to the directories or files to be listed.
- **Pipes**: These are used for linking the output of one or more commands as input to other commands.
- **Lists**: These enable users to run multiple commands in sequence.
- **Compound commands**: This command allows script programming and contains loops for repeating a command, a specific number of times and conditional constructs for running commands only when specific conditions are met.

Learn key troubleshooting and debugging skills to apply to your projects

Troubleshooting and debugging are very important as every programmer cannot fully escape bugs from their program code. For this reason, every programmer ought to know the basic troubleshooting and debugging skills necessary and needed to get rid of bugs in their programs. There are three major ways to deal with bugs:

1. Pre-bugging: This is an action taken to reduce bugs before they're created.
2. Debugging: This is the process of recognizing, fixing, and eliminating bugs once you find them.
3. Post-debugging: This prepares you to be expecting unexpected or unknown bugs after the previous steps have been observed.

The following steps discuss some of the ways you can avoid bugs from your project:

1. Engage in proper planning before starting to code.
2. Learn to write program specs.
3. Learn to understand or study the tools you use.
4. Learn to type accurately as some of the programming codes are case sensitive.
5. Familiarize yourself with error messages and their probable solutions. Both the Syntax Errors, Logic/Semantic Errors, Compilation Errors, Resource Errors, and Interface Errors.

6. You should also learn to watch fellow developers while debugging.

How to Understand Why Bugs Occur

After finding a bug in your program, you need to find out why the code is acting the way it does. Doing this helps you build an efficient debugging competence. Instead many developers will just go ahead to google it and use the answers they get directly from Stack Overflow and other platforms. That is cool in certain conditions, but it is better to understand the cause of a bug and why the solution works.

Understanding the source or root cause of a bug is an important step on the path of debugging, to fixing it or removing the bug.

How to Fix or Remove Bugs

After the discovery and understanding of the reason why a bug occurs, you have to fix the bug. At times, once you understand what the bug is, you'll simply find a solution without stress. However, there are times when our understanding produces no solution no matter how tough we try. Instead of wasting time and energy, it is okay to Google the error message or whatsoever you feel is suitable. You can also ask fellow developers or get to ask for solutions to the bugs you encounter in any of the developer's communities because others tend to see things differently. They are neutral and that neutrality does help in fixing some bugs most times.

CHAPTER THREE

FRONT-END DEVELOPMENT

HTML is the standard mark-up language for creating a Web page

The abbreviation HTML stands for Hyper Text Markup Language. It's the standard markup language for creating Web pages, HTML describes the structure of a Web page which consists of a series of elements. These elements tell the browser how to display those HTML contents. HTML elements label pieces of content such as; this is a section, this is a paragraph, this is a heading, "this is a link", etc.

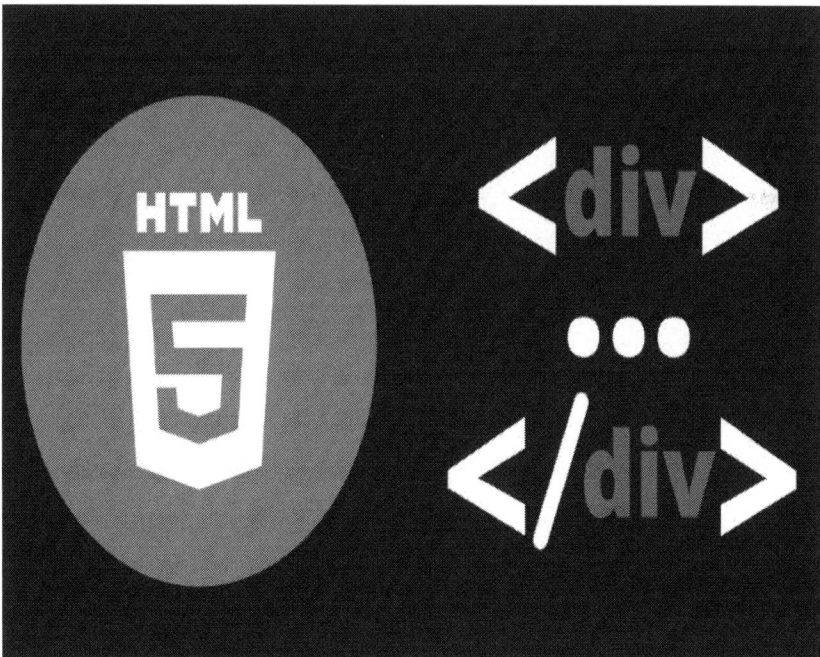

A Simple HTML Document

A simple HTML document consists of all the components of HTML code which include all the elements, starting from the doctype to attributes and properties of a single HTML code. See the screenshot below showing a simple HTML5 document.

```
Terminal  Help                    ● example.html - Nmadu Samuel Internship - Visual Studio Code

 Get Started      ◇ index.html      ◇ example.html ●

◇ example.html > ⬦ html
 1   <!DOCTYPE html>
 2   <html lang="en">
 3   <head>
 4       <meta charset="UTF-8">
 5       <meta http-equiv="X-UA-Compatible" content="IE=edge">
 6       <meta name="viewport" content="width=device-width, initial-scale=1.0">
 7       <title>Page Title</title>
 8   </head>
 9   <body>
10
11   <h1>My First Heading</h1>
12   <p>My first paragraph.</p>
13
14   </body>
15   </html>
```

The screenshot above is further explained in the following points:

- The <!DOCTYPE html> declaration shows that the said HTML document is an HTML5 document. Though that section mostly defines the version of HTML you are implementing.

39

- The <html> tag encloses all the elements of an HTML page or it's said to be the root element of an HTML page. This means that all HTML elements must be within the tag.
- The <head> tag section comprises all the meta-information about the HTML page.
- The <title> tag section specifies a title for the HTML page which is usually displayed in the browser's title bar or the page's tab.
- The <body> tag section describes the document's body, it's a holder for all the seeable contents, such as headings, hyperlinks, paragraphs, lists, images, tables, and other HTML contents.
- The <h1> tag section defines a large heading or heading 1 because the headings range from heading 1 to heading 6.
- The <p> tag section defines a paragraph and its contents.

What is an HTML Element?

An HTML element is defined by a start tag, followed by some content, and then the end or close tag. The HTML **element** is all from the start tag to the end tag. See the syntax and some examples below.

<tag name> The Content goes here! </tag name>

1. <h1>My First Heading</h1>
2. <p>My first paragraph.</p>

(NB: Some HTML tags are self-closing tags. And those elements have no content, elements like the <br>, <hr>, <img> and other elements). These elements are called empty elements. Empty elements do not have an end tag).

Understanding basic software tools needed

The following are the basic software tools needed for every starter, to begin with.

1. Text editors software: Text editors software are a computer program that lets a user enter, change, store, and usually print text, that is, characters and numbers, each encoded by the computer and its input and output devices, thy are organized to have meaning to users or other programs.

2. Modern web browser software: Web browsers are computer software application that enables a person or users to locate, retrieve, and display content such as webpages, images, video, as well as other files on the World Wide Web.

Install a text editor

You perhaps already have a basic text editor on your computer. By default Windows OS contains Notepad, macOS by default also comes with TextEdit. Linux distros vary, and Ubuntu comes with gedit by default. But others can be installed because you will be using them to write and execute your codes. The following are some of the best text editors you can use.

- Visual Studio Code.

- Atom.

- Sublime Text.

- Notepad++, etc.

Install a modern web browsers

The following are the modern web browser you can use to test your code, but it varies across the different operating systems.

- For **Linux**: You can search and download Firefox, Chrome, Opera, Brave, etc.

- For **Windows**: You can search and download Firefox, Chrome, Opera, Internet Explorer, Microsoft Edge, Brave, etc. Though Windows 10 comes with Microsoft Edge by default. But, if you have Windows 7 or above, you can install Internet Explorer; if not, you should install other browsers.

- For **macOS**: Firefox, Chrome, Safari, Opera, Brave, etc. macOS and iOS also come with Safari by default.

- Before you proceed, you should install at least two of these browsers and have them ready for program testing.

NB: Internet Explorer is not compatible with some modern web features and it may not be able to run your project or gives you the required output. I suggest you use either Chrome or Firefox to test your programs.

Learn the anatomy of HTML syntax to structure your websites

The anatomy of HTML syntax implies that you learn the structure or various elements and components that makeup HTML code. Understand how to use them, and their functions or usage. HTML which means Hypertext Markup Language is the code that is used to structure a web page and its content. For instance, content could be structured inside a set of paragraphs, a list of bulleted points, or using images, data tables, and other allowable HTML components. This anatomy implies that you understand HTML Basic, HTML Form, HTML Graphics, HTML Media and HTML APIs:

HTML Basic

HTML Basics consist of the following:

HTML Elements, HTML Attributes, HTML Headings, HTML Paragraphs, HTML Styles, HTML Formatting, HTML Quotations, HTML Comments, HTML Colors, HTML CSS, HTML Links, HTML Images, HTML Favicon, HTML Tables, HTML Lists, HTML Block & Inline, HTML Classes, HTML Id, HTML Iframes, HTML JavaScript, HTML File Paths, HTML Head, HTML Layout, HTML Responsive, HTML Semantics, HTML Style Guide, HTML Entities, HTML Symbols, HTML

Emojis, HTML Charset, HTML URL Encode, and HTML vs. XHTML.

HTML Forms

HTML Forms, HTML Form Attributes, HTML Form Elements, HTML Input Types, HTML Input Attributes, and HTML Input Form Attributes.

HTML Graphics

HTML Canvas, and HTML SVG.

HTML Media

HTML Media, HTML Video, HTML Audio, HTML Plug-ins, and HTML YouTube.

HTML APIs

HTML Geolocation, HTML Drag/Drop, HTML Web Storage, HTML Web Workers, and HTML SSE

Understand the HTML boilerplate and HTML doctypes

HTML boilerplate is a code in form of a template that every developer must use to create an HTML document. This beginner's code comprises important information like the doctype, metadata, external stylesheet script tags, and other components. Boilerplate code or just boilerplate consists of divisions of code that are repeated in several places with little to no differences. A boilerplate in HTML is a template you will add at the start of your program. You ought to add this boilerplate to all of your HTML pages.

The screenshot below is an example of an HTML 5 **Boilerplate**.

```
Run  Terminal  Help                    • example.html - Nmadu Samuel Internship - Visual Studio Code

 ··  ◢ Get Started      ◇ index.html      ◇ example.html •

     ◇ example.html > ⊗ html > ⊗ body > ⊗ script
      1   <!DOCTYPE html>
      2   <html lang="en">
      3   <head>
      4       <meta charset="UTF-8">
      5       <meta http-equiv="X-UA-Compatible" content="IE=edge">
      6       <meta name="viewport" content="width=device-width, initial-scale=1.0">
      7       <title>HTML 5 boilerPlate</title>
      8   </head>
      9   <body>
     10       <script src="index.js"></script>
     11
     12   </body>
     13   </html>
```

The DOCTYPE in HTML

The opening line of your HTML code contains the Doctype declaration. A Doctype tells the browser the version of HTML your code is written in. If you forget to include this line of code in your file, then some of the HTML 5 tags like

45

<footer>, <header>, and <article>, may not be compatible or supported by the browser. The following is the HTML 5 doctype declaration.

<!DOCTYPE html>

The HTML root element

The <html> tag is one of the paramount and first-level elements of the HTML file. The <head> and <body> tags are usually nested inside of it.

See the example below showing the HTML root element and

<html lang="en">

  <head></head>

<body></body>

</html>

The lang attribute within the opening <html> tag defines the language for the page. It is also good to include it for accessibility reasons because screen readers will know how to appropriately read out the text.

What are head tags in HTML?

The <head> tags hold data that is processed by machines. Inside the <head> tags, is nested metadata which is data that defines the document to the machine. See the example below showing the head tags and their contents.

```
<head>

  <meta charset="UTF-8">

  <meta  name="viewport"  content="width=device-width,
initial-scale=1.0">

  <meta http-equiv="X-UA-Compatible" content="ie=edge">

  <title>HTML 5 Boilerplate</title>

  <link rel="stylesheet" href="style.css">

</head>
```

What is UTF-8 character encoding?

The UTF-8 is the standard and acceptable character encoding you ought to use on your web pages. This is usually the first <meta> tag displayed in the <head> element.

See the example below.

```
<meta charset="UTF-8">
```

Concerning the World Wide Web Consortium, A Unicode-based encoding such as UTF-8 can allow many languages and can house pages and forms in any combination of those languages. Using it eliminates the need for server-side logic to personally determine the character encoding for separate pages served or each incoming form submission.

What is the viewport meta tag in HTML?

The viewport meta tag defines the width of the page to the width of your device's screen size. When you have a mobile device that is 600px wide, then the browser window must also be 600px wide.

The initial scale manages the zoom level. The value of 1 for the initial scale avoids the default zoom by browsers. See the example below.

```
<meta name="viewport" content="width=device-width, initial-scale=1.0">
```

What does X-UA-Compatible mean?

The X-UA <meta> tag defines the document mode for your Internet Explorer. IE=edge is the utmost supported mode. See the example below.

```
<meta http-equiv="X-UA-Compatible" content="ie=edge">
```

What are HTML title tags?

The <title> tag specifies the title for the web page. The HTML 5 Boilerplate text represents the title that will be seen in the browser's title bar as depicted in the example below.

```
<title>HTML 5 Boilerplate</title>
```

CSS stylesheet

The CSS stylesheet code below, when implemented will link your custom CSS to the HTML page. The rel="stylesheet" defines the connection between the HTML file and the external stylesheet.

<link rel="stylesheet" href="style.css">

Script tags in HTML

The External script tags will be positioned just before the closing body tag. This is where you can link your external JavaScript code. See the example below.

<script src="index.js"></script>

The HTML Doctypes

All HTML documents must begin with a <!DOCTYPE> declaration. This is because you must define the version of the HTML document type that you are using.

This declaration is regarded as an HTML tag. But it's information to your browser about what document type to display the page content.

In HTML5, the <!DOCTYPE> declaration is as shown in the example below:

<!DOCTYPE html>

In other documents type such as HTML 4 or XHTML, the declaration is more complex because the declaration must reference a DTD (Document Type Definition).

Below is an example of an HTML 4 document type declaration.

- <!DOCTYPE HTML PUBLIC "-//W3C//DTD HTML 4.01 Transitional//EN" "http://www.w3.org/TR/html4/loose.dtd">

Below is an example of an XHTML document type declaration.

- <!DOCTYPE html PUBLIC "-//W3C//DTD XHTML 1.1//EN" "http://www.w3.org/TR/xhtml11/DTD/xhtml11.dtd">

How to structure text in HTML

On a Web page, the content is organized into different formats, such as tables, layers, lines, paragraphs, and divisions. Structuring of text in HTML refers to the accurate placement of all the HTML tags and their content on a Web page. As a practice, by omitting line and paragraph breaks, a web browser wraps content within a web page and presents the encapsulated text as a single block. Now, if a page's contents also aren't broken up into any line or paragraph divisions, it might be very difficult for readers to comprehend the given information. If the text on the Web page is not arranged then the readers will find difficulty reading the desired information.

You can arrange the text in several ways, such as paragraphs, lines, and tables, to solve this issue. A variety of tags are available in HTML to divide content into paragraphs and tables. For instance, you can use the P element to show the text on the Website page as paragraphs or use a horizontal line to indicate a text break. The SPAN tag in HTML also enables you to change the format of a certain text.

How to structure HTML lists to create unordered and ordered lists

Unordered list: The <ul> tag is the first part of an HTML unordered list structure. The <li> tag also marked the start of the list item. The list items will be automatically marked with bullet information of tiny black circles at the output. Check out the code below to see how the HTML for unordered lists is structured.

```
<ul>
  <li>Bread</li>
  <li>Tea</li>
  <li>Butter</li>
</ul>
```

Ordered List: An ordered list HTML structure starts with the <ol> tag. And the <li> tag appears at the beginning of each list item. The output will by default mark the list items with numbers. Check out the code below to see how the HTML for unordered lists is structured.

```
<ol>
  <li>Coffee</li>
  <li>Tea</li>
  <li>Milk</li>
</ol>
```

How to insert images using HTML

An image can be added to a web page using the HTML <img> tag. Images are integrated into web pages; they are not placed into web pages. The relevant picture is held in place using the <img> tag. The image tag has no ending tag, is empty, and only includes attributes.

The <img> tag has two required attributes:

- Src: This specifies the path to the image.
- Alt: This specifies an alternate text for the image.

<img src="url" alt="alternatetext">

How to create hyperlinks using anchor tags

Hyperlinks are links in HTML. You can access another document by clicking on a link. The mouse arrow will change into a tiny hand when you move the mouse pointer over a link. The HTML <a> tag defines a hyperlink. The href attribute of the <a> element, which denotes the location of the link, is its most crucial component. The portion that the reader will see is the link text. The reader will be directed to the provided URL address by clicking on the link text.

This example shows how to create a link to Amazon.com:

<a href="https://www.amazon.com">Visit Amazon!</a>

```
   File  Edit  Selection  View  Go  Run  Terminal  Help        ● contact.html - Visual Studio Code
   <> contact.html ●      JS index.js    ●      # index2.css 2 ●
   C: > Web Design > web > <> contact.html > ⊘ html > ⊘ body > ⊘ p
   1     <!DOCTYPE html>
   2     <html lang="en">
   3     <head>
   4       <meta charset="UTF-8">
   5       <meta http-equiv="X-UA-Compatible" content="IE=edge">
   6       <meta name="viewport" content="width=device-width, initial-scale=1.0">
   7       <title>Document</title>
   8     </head>
   9     <body>
   10
   11        <h1>HTML Links</h1>
   12
   13        <p><a href="https://www.amazon.com/">Visit Amazon.com!</a></p>
   14
   15    </body>
   16    </html>
```

Understand how to use HTML tables for content

An HTML table consists of cells arranged in rows and columns. Tables also consist of a table head or header. Individual table cell is well-defined by a <td> and a </td> tag that is, the opening and the closing tag. While td stands for table data. The whole thing between <td> and </td> is the information of the table cell.

A table also consists of a table row that starts with a <tr> and closes with a </tr> tag. While tr stands for table row. At times you may want your cells to be headers, in such cases, you should use the <th> tag in place of the <td> tag.

See the screenshot below showing how you can implement the properties discussed earlier.

53

```
<table>
  <tr>
    <th>Company</th>
    <th>Contact</th>
    <th>Country</th>
  </tr>
  <tr>
    <td>Alfreds Futterkiste</td>
    <td>Maria Anders</td>
    <td>Germany</td>
  </tr>
  <tr>
    <td>Centro comercial Moctezuma</td>
    <td>Francisco Chang</td>
    <td>Mexico</td>
  </tr>
</table>
```

How to use tables for layout

The algorithm used to lay up table cells, rows, and columns are defined by the table-layout attribute. The biggest advantage of table layout: especially fixed; is that the table renders significantly faster. Users can not view any part of the table till the browser has processed the entire table. Users would see the top of the table while the browser loads and renders the rest of the table if you set table-layout: fixed. This leaves the notion that the page loads much faster.

See the screenshot below showing the syntax for using a table for layout:

```
table.a {
    table-layout:  auto;
    width:  180px;
}

table.b {
    table-layout:  fixed;
    width:  180px;
}
```

The screenshot below shows the Layout property values and description for the table layout:

Value	Description
Auto	Browsers use an automatic table layout algorithm. The column width is set by the widest unbreakable content in the cells. The content will dictate the layout.
Fixed	Sets a fixed table layout algorithm. The table and column widths are set by the widths of table and col or by the width of the first row of cells. Cells in other rows do not affect column widths. If no widths are present on the first row, the column widths are divided equally across the table, regardless of content inside the cells.
Initial	This option sets this property to its default value.
Inherit	This Inherits the said property from its parent element.

Learn HTML best practices

HTML best practices are guidelines that assist you in creating websites that are simple to handle and use. The following are some of the guiding principles to keep in mind when building an HTML-based website.

1. **Use proper document structure:** HTML documents will continue to function without elements such like <html>, <head>, and <body>. Nevertheless, because the pages will not display correctly across every browser, it is critical to use a consistent document structure.

See the screenshot below showing the HTML5 document structure.

```
<!DOCTYPE html>
<html>
<head>
        <title>Hello World</title>
</head>
<body>

        <h1>Welcome</h1>
        <p>This is a website.</p>

</body>
</html>
```

2. **Declare the correct doctype:** The first item to declare when creating an HTML document is the doctype. This tells the browser the standards you're utilizing to produce your markup properly. At the top of the page,

56

the doctype comes before the <html> tag. If you are unclear about which declaration to use, W3.org has guidance on selecting the appropriate doctype.

3. **Always close tags:** To avoid validation issues, please remember to include a closing tag for each tag you create, except for the self-closing tags.

4. **Don't use inline styles:** It may appear to be a simple solution to include styling in the code rather than establishing an external style sheet. Nevertheless, style sheets are not a smart coding practice because they make updating and maintaining a website more difficult. Hold your styles distinct from your HTML markup instead.

5. **Use alt attribute with images:** Because an alt attribute is not necessary for every image, it is easy to overlook. However, a relevant alt attribute is required for validation and accessibility. Screen readers rely on the alt element for context, therefore it should be descriptive of the image's contents.

6. **Validate frequently:** Rather than waiting until you've finished your HTML document, inspect it several times as you go. It will save time and stress by discovering errors immediately, particularly if your document is extensive. W3C's markup validation service is a common HTML validator to utilize.

7. **Place external style sheets within the <head> tag:** Even though external style sheets can be inserted anywhere within the HTML text, it is recommended that they are included within the <head> tag. This will speed up the loading of your page.

8. **Use meaningful tags:** The most suitable HTML5 tag for the content should be used to construct each component of your website. It's recommended to refrain from using generic tags like "div" when more specialized tags like "section" or "article" would be more applicable.

9. **Use lowercase markup:** The web page will render appropriately whether lowercase or uppercase letters are used in your HTML markup. But since it is simpler to understand and manage, it is a recommended practice to keep tag names in lowercase.

10. **Reduce the number of elements on a page:** Particularly for websites with a lot of material, HTML documents could become difficult. Once your markup is complete, look for chances to further optimize your code to make your pages smaller.

Understand HTML forms and create a simple contact me form

An HTML form for user input is made using the HTML "form" element. The most popular form element is the HTML "input" element. Relying on the type attribute, there are various ways that an <input> element can be shown.

See the syntax below showing how you can create a simple contact me form.

```
File    Edit    Selection    View    Go    Run    Terminal    Help              • contact.html - Visual Studio Code

<> contact.html •
C: > Web Design > web > <> contact.html > <> html > <> body > <> form > <> div#f
  1    <!DOCTYPE html>
  2    <html>
  3    <head>
  4        <title>Online Career Portal</title>
  5        <link rel="stylesheet" type="text/css" href="index.CSS">
  6    </head>
  7    <body>
  8      <form>
  9    <div id="left">
 10        <h1 align="center">  CONTACT US</h1>
 11    </div>
 12    <div id="f">
 13        <label for="fullname">Full Name:</label>
 14        <input type="text" name="fullname" required>
 15    </div> <br></br>
 16    <div id="f">
 17        <label for="email">Email:</label>
 18        <input type="text" name="email" id="email" required>
 19    </div>
 20    <br></br>
 21    <div id="f">
 22        <label for="phonenumber"> Number:</label>
 23        <input type="text" name="phonenumber" id="phonenumber" required>
 24    </div>
 25    <br></br>
 26    <div id="f">
 27    <label for="message">Message:</label><br></br>
 28    <textarea rows="10" cols="50"></textarea>
 29    <input type="submit" name="submit" id="submit" value="Send" />
 30    <input type="reset" name="reset" id="reset" value="Reset" />
 31    </div></div>
 32     </form></body>
 33    </html>
```

HTML Divs and how to separate content for CSS styling

The HTML division tag, typically known as "div", it's a unique element that enables you to bring together pieces of related material on a web page. It can serve as a general container for linking together stuff that is related. Despite the advent of semantic elements, the div tag remains one of the most used tags and doesn't seem to be declining in popularity (these elements let you use several tags as a container).

The div tag is multifunctional; you may use it on a web page to do a variety of tasks. It's adaptable, although you'll usually use it in web setups and CSS art. In the end, you'll nearly always use it to style the content or use JavaScript to change it. The div tag is typically used to group similar content so that styling it is simple. Using div to organize various homepage components into groups is a fantastic illustration of this. A page's header, navigation, sections, and footer can all be combined into one div tag so they can be designed as a single unit. Unless you style it, div itself has no direct impact on how the content is shown.

See the screenshot below showing how you can implement the div tag in HTML.

CHAPTER THREE

UNDERSTANDING C S S 3

Understanding Cascading Style Sheets and how you can use them to style your website

Cascading Style Sheets is a language for creating style sheets that describe how a document is presented in a markup language, such as HTML or XML. The World Wide Web's foundational technology, used along with HTML and JavaScript is CSS.

The language we employ to style a Web page is CSS. CSS is also known as Cascading Style Sheets, style sheet is a great method of organizing the presentation of HTML elements on screens, paper, and other media or platforms. External stylesheets are saved in CSS files and can be used to alter the layout of numerous web pages simultaneously. Your web pages' design, layout, and differences in display for various devices and screen sizes are all styled using CSS.

Since CSS is a language with rules, you establish the rules by identifying sets of styles that should be used on particular elements or sets of elements on your website. CSS has a simple syntax. A selector, a property, a value, and then a declaration block follows.

For instance, you might determine that the primary header, the body, and a paragraph should all be structured using the correct syntax. See the screenshot below showing how you can implement that.

```
body {
    background-color: lightblue;
}

h1 {
    color: white;
    text-align: center;
}

p {
    font-family: verdana;
    font-size: 20px;
}
```

Learn how to use CSS selectors and roperties

The element that has to be styled is called a selector. Selectors, however, are more than just elements, as you'll find out when you create more CSS code. They might be ids, classes, pseudo-classes, attributes, or descendants.

The HTML components you want to style are "identified" or selected using CSS selectors. All of the <p> elements on the page will be center-aligned and have red text in this example of a CSS element selector.

```
p {
    text-align: center;
    color: red;
}
```

We can divide CSS selectors into five categories:

- Basic selectors (select elements based on name, id, class)
- Selectors for combinators (select elements based on a specific relationship between them).
- Pseudo-class selectors (select elements based on a certain state).
- Selectors for pseudo-elements (select and style a part of an element).
- Attribute selectors (select elements based on an attribute or attribute value).

"CSS selectors identify the elements on an HTML page that match patterns described in a selector and apply style rules that adhere to the selector to those selected elements," according to W3resource.

The syntax for using any of the selectors is the same as CSS basic syntax.

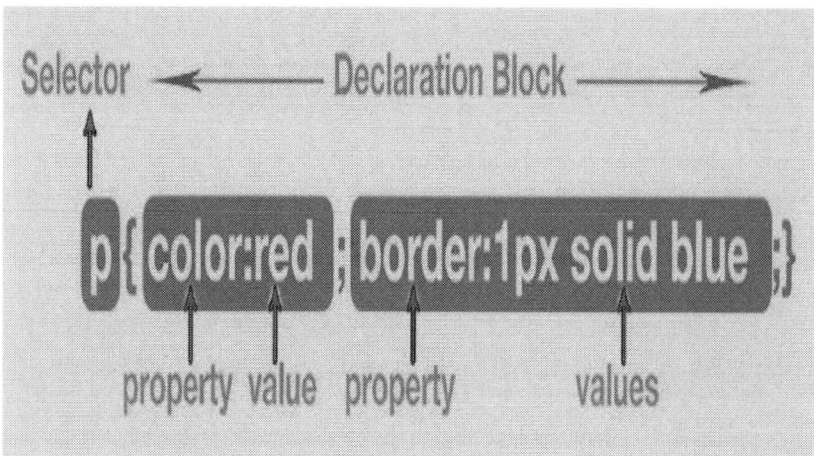

CSS Properties

The styles applied to certain selectors via CSS are known as properties. They are listed before values and a colon separates them from property values in the CSS ruleset. The properties of various HTML selectors and components vary. Several properties apply to all selectors and are universal. Others only function with certain selections and under certain circumstances.

Grid-template-columns, which are used to style the page's layout, is an example of it. It primarily functions with divs whose displayed property is set to the grid (display: grid).

HTML selectors have a large number of properties and their values. There are "520 different property names from 66 technical reports and 66 editor's drafts," according to CSS Tricks.

Below are four common properties to work with in

- List properties.
- Font properties.
- Border properties.
- Text properties.

Because they may be applied to various selectors and are often used in all CSS texts, these properties are widely used. Properties have the distinction of having several values associated with them. For instance, the property text-transform, which determines how a text is capitalized, can be set to uppercase, lowercase, capitalize, or none. But there is a constraint here as well. If the correct property is not given to a value, nothing happens. Nothing will change in the text portion if we specify "text-transform: underline;" because underline is a value for text-decoration.

Several properties, their descriptions, and the values they support are listed below.

Learn about how to use inline, internal, and external CSS

Three methods exist for adding CSS in HTML. To style a single HTML element on the page, you can include inline CSS in the style attribute. By including CSS in the head part of your HTML document, you can embed an internal stylesheet. Alternatively, you can connect to an external stylesheet that houses all your CSS independently from your HTML.

Here's another way to summarize the three options for including CSS in HTML:

- Inline CSS: Necessitates the placement of the style attribute inside an HTML element.
- Internal CSS: Necessitates the insertion of the <style> element inside the head area of an HTML file.
- External CSS: Needs to have the link> element in the HTML file's head section.

The best use cases for each way of introducing CSS to HTML are discussed below.

How to Add Inline CSS to HTML

You can include CSS "in" HTML by using inline CSS. You utilize a style attribute and insert it within the opening tag of an HTML element to add inline CSS. Here is how to use it:

```
<element style="CSS property: value">
```

How to Add Internal CSS to HTML

Inline CSS appears one way, and internal CSS looks another. A CSS property and value are still set, but now they are enclosed in brackets and defined by a CSS selector rather than being contained within a style attribute. The head part of the HTML file contains this rule set once it has been enclosed in tags. It is recommended to use internal CSS rather than inline CSS.

Instead of repeatedly adding the same style attributes to elements, internal CSS enables you to style groups of elements at once.

Additionally, internal CSS is perfect for one-page websites since it divides the HTML and CSS into distinct sections while keeping them in the same document. If your website consists of multiple pages and you want to make changes to them all, you must open each HTML file for those pages and add or modify the internal CSS in each head section.

```
<!DOCTYPE html>

<html>

<head>

<style>

p {

  color: #33475B;

}

</style>

</head>

<body>

<h2>Internal CSS Example</h2>

<p>The default text color for the page is black. However

<p>Using internal CSS, I only need to write one rule set

<p>With inline CSS, I'd have to add a style attribute to

</body>

</html>
```

How to Add an External CSS File to HTML

External CSS is formatted similarly to internal CSS, it isn't contained within <style> tags or added to the HTML file's head section. It is instead stored in an external file with the .css extension. You only need to include a link to this external stylesheet in the head section, something like:

```
<link rel="stylesheet" type="text/css" rel="noopener" target="_blank" href="mystyles.css">
```

Using external CSS is considered the best practice for a few reasons.

It's the fastest option because you may alter the CSS in this external file and apply it to your entire website. Additionally, it is the quickest and SEO-friendly. Your HTML page will be simpler for search engines to read if CSS is stored in a separate file. Additionally, it makes it possible for a visitor's browser to store the CSS file to speed up their subsequent visits to your website.

```
<!DOCTYPE html>

<html>

<head>

<link rel="stylesheet" type="text/css" rel="noopener" tar

</head>

<body>

<div>

<h1>External CSS Example</h1>

<p>In the external stylesheet, the div is styled to have

</div>

</body>

</html>
```

Understand CSS coding best practices

You must comprehend a few terminology and concepts to use CSS best practices correctly. Below is a list of important CSS terms and their definitions to help you get up to speed.

1. **CSS files**: A CSS file is a document that is added to a web development project and contains the CSS rules that describe how a site should look.
2. **CSS selectors**: In a line of CSS code, a CSS selector is often the first element. It serves to identify to which HTML element the code is referring in the browser. Simple selectors, attribute selectors, combinator selectors, pseudo-class selectors, and pseudo-elements selectors are the five different categories of CSS selectors.
3. **CSS classes**: To bring together several HTML components and apply the same styling and formatting, use a CSS class.
4. **Declaration blocks**: CSS code lines surrounded by curly brackets are known as declaration blocks. Each block's attributes and values are separated from one another by colons, and the declarations are separated from one another by semicolons.
5. **Inline styles**: Inline styles are used in CSS programming to apply formatting and style rules to a single HTML element. The HTML tag should include the inline style code.
6. **External stylesheets**: It's excellent practice in web development to use external stylesheets rather than

inline styles. All of the CSS code needed to format and style a web page is included in stylesheets, which are documents. The head section of an HTML document contains the link to an external stylesheet. You can make adjustments that apply to the entire website rather than just a particular page by using an external stylesheet.

7. **Embedded styles:** Embedded styles are placed inside the HTML document's head section. They only have an impact on the page in which they are contained, in contrast to external stylesheets.

8. **CSS frameworks:** A CSS framework is a collection of pre-written, standard-compliant code that facilitates the creation of interactive, responsive web pages and web applications.

9. **CSS compressors:** CSS compressors are outside programs used to make CSS code files smaller. Compressors are used to increase a website or application's capacity for growth. To speed up loading and boost performance, it removes the CSS code's non-functional components such as spaces, comments, and indentations.

10. **Inheritance:** In CSS programming, inheritance refers to a rule that determines what value is assigned to a property in the absence of a specified value. Non-inherited properties adopt the initial value of the property, whereas inherited properties take on the value of the parent element.

Learn about CSS sizing methods

We can incorporate padding and border in an element's overall width and height thanks to the CSS box-sizing feature. Any element that accepts a width or height can have its size changed or controlled using the CSS box-sizing attribute. It details how to determine the element's overall width and height. Two div elements with the same width and height may be seen in the code snippet below, however, the first div seems to be larger than the second div.

Any element that accepts a width or height in the following format is calculated by the CSS box model by default:

- width + padding + border = rendered or displayed width of the element's box.
- height + padding + border = rendered or displayed height of the element's box.

This implies that the size of an element will appear larger than the size that was initially assigned to it whenever padding or border are added to the element. This is so because the width and height properties are included in the content of that element, but not the padding or border properties.

```
.first-box {
  width: 200px;
  height: 100px;
  border: 8px solid blue;
  padding: 20px;
  background: yellow;
  /* Total width: 200px + (2 * 20px) + (2 * 8px) = 256px
     Total height: 100px + (2 * 20px) + (2 * 8px) = 156px */
}

.second-box {
  width: 200px;
  height: 100px;
  border: 8px solid blue;
  background: yellow;
  /* Total width: 200px + (2 * 8px) = 216px
     Total height: 100px +  (2 * 8px) = 116px */
}
```

Learn the anatomy of CSS syntax and structure

A selector, a property, and its value are the components of a CSS Syntax rule. The HTML element where CSS style is to be applied is indicated by the selector. Semicolons are used to separate each CSS property. The property, value pair that is specified for the particular selector is combined with the selection name.

A CSS rule consists of a selector and a declaration block as shown below:

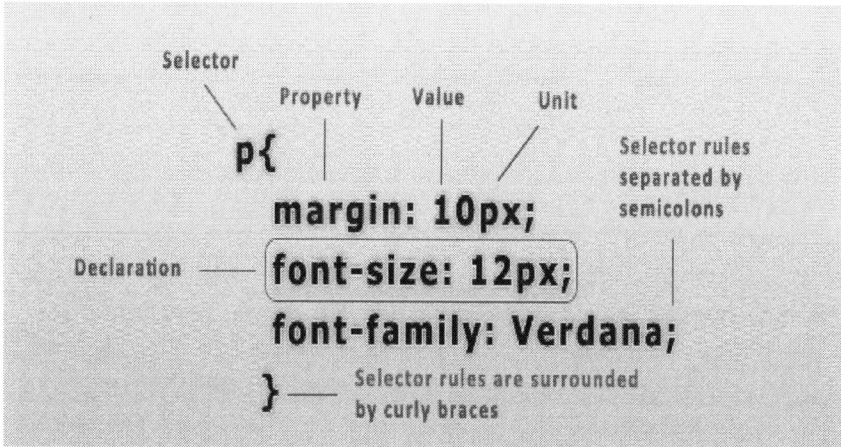

The CSS structure basics, from rulesets to values and units:

- Declarations.
- Properties.
- Selectors.
- Rules or rulesets.
- Values and units.

CSS specificity and implementing style hierarchy

The browser must choose which specific set of CSS rules will be applied to an element when multiple sets of CSS rules apply to the same object. The set of guidelines the browser adheres to is referred to as **Specificity**.

Specificity Rules include:

- Internal and inline CSS take precedence over CSS styles applied by referencing an external stylesheet since they have a higher priority.

- Inline CSS takes precedence over internal CSS.
- All other selectors are superseded and given lower priority by inline CSS.

Specificity Hierarchy:

Every element selector has a position in the Hierarchy.

1. **Inline style:** Inline formatting is given top precedence.
2. **Identifiers (ID):** The second highest priority is given to ID.
3. **Classes, pseudo-classes, and attributes:** These three categories come next.
4. **Elements and pseudo-elements:** These entities are given the least amount of priority.

See the example below:

```
<html>

<head>
    <link rel="stylesheet" type="text/css" href="external.css">
    <style type="text/css">
        h1 {
            background-color: red;
            color: white;
        }

        h2 {
            color: blue;
        }
    </style>
</head>

<body>
    <h1>
        Internal CSS overrides external CSS
    </h1>
    <h2 style="color: green;">
        Inline CSS overrides internal CSS
    </h2>
</body>

</html>
```

Class vs. IDs and how to target each CSS display and how to implement layout

CSS uses class and ID selectors to categorize different HTML components. Setting class or ID has the main advantage of allowing you to present the same HTML element in several ways depending on its class or ID. A class selector in CSS is a name preceded by a period (".") character, and an ID selector is a name preceded by a hash ("#") character.

Class selector

A specific class attribute is used by the class selector to choose elements. Based on the information included in their class attribute, it matches every HTML element. To choose the desired class, enter the class name and the symbol.

See the screenshot below:

```
1  .class-name {
2      /* Define properties here */
3  }
```

ID selector

Based on the value of an element's id attribute, the ID selector matches it. The ID property of the element must exactly match the value entered in the selector for it to be selected.

The required HTML element is selected using the # sign and the element's ID name.

```
1   #idname {
2       /* Define properties here */
3   }
```

(NB: They are used to implement layout by specifying or adding properties to both of them in your CSS code).

The difference between Class and ID selector

An ID is different from a class in that it can only be used to identify a particular element in our HTML. IDs are only employed when a specific style should be applied to a single element on the page. However, more than one HTML element can be identified using a class.

How to use CSS static, relative, and absolute positioning systems

In the CSS position property, an element's position within a document is determined by a CSS attribute. The ultimate positions of elements that have been placed depend on their top, right, bottom, and left characteristics.

The CSS positioning properties are as follows:

```
position: static;

position: relative;

position: absolute;
```

1. Static

The default setting for an element is static positioning. This means that if a position is not declared for an element in CSS, it will default to static. Note that having a static position is equivalent to never set the position attribute. (This will be relevant when discussing absolute placement later.)

The regular flow, as we like to call it, will be followed by elements that are statically positioned on the page. For instance, if you place several <div> components side by side on the page, they will all display underneath one another.

2. Relative

Position: Similar to static positioning, relative positioning allows items to follow the website's normal flow. The use of relative will now enable the additional CSS layout attributes, however, that is the primary change.

3. Absolute

Absolute positioning will cause an element to be removed from the web page's normal flow. Therefore, depending on their sequence in the HTML code, items would previously be attractively presented one below the other using static or relative placement. But with absolute positioning, the element is taken out of that entire flow.

See the following screenshot shows how to use the three of the types of positions mostly used in CSS.

```
Terminal   Help                    • index2.css - Visual S

<> contact.html  •        #  index2.css  •

C: > Web Design > web > # index2.css > t3 .t
  1
  2      .first {
  3          position: static;
  4      }
  5      .second {
  6          position: relative;
  7          top: 50px;
  8
  9      }
 10      .third {
 11          position: absolute;
 12          bottom: 50px;
 13
 14
 15      }
```

(NB: There are several other positioning types but just these three are discussed here, but you can explore others).

Font styling using CSS and web-safe fonts

In font-style CSS property design, a font rendering font family determines whether it should be styled with a regular, italic, or oblique face.

The CSS attributes that are often used to style text may be divided into two groups, each of the groups is discussed below:

- Font styles: Font style properties may affect fonts by several factors, including the font's size, boldness, italicization, and other attributes.
- Text layout styles: These contain the attributes that modify the spacing and other text layout aspects. For instance, they let change the distance between lines and characters as well as how the text is oriented within the content box.

There are a certain number of fonts that are usually available across all devices and can consequently be used without much worry. They are called **web-safe fonts**.

What Is a Web-Safe Font?

Most operating systems come with pre-installed fonts that are web-safe. This guarantees that the fonts display as intended across a range of platforms and browsers.

The most well-known examples of web-safe fonts include Helvetica, Times New Roman, and Arial.

```
<> contact.html  ●      #  index2.css  ●

C: > Web Design > web > # index2.css > ᵺ .oblique
  1
  2     .normal {
  3         font-style: normal;
  4     }
  5
  6     .italic {
  7         font-style: italic;
  8     }
  9
 10     .oblique {
 11         font-style: oblique;
 12     }
```

Centering elements using CSS

Use margin: auto to horizontally center a block element such as <div>;

Setting the element's width will stop it from encroaching on the borders of its container. Following that, the element will fill the designated width and the leftover space will be evenly divided between the two margins. Use text-align: center to simply center the text inside an element.

```css
<> contact.html  •      # index2.css  •
C: > Web Design > web > # index2.css > 🔁 .child
 1    /* Text Alignment*/
 2    .center
 3    {
 4        text-align: center;
 5    }
 6    /* Element Alignment*/
 7    .center
 8    {
 9        margin: 0 auto;
10        width: 200px;
11    }
12    /*Aligning Multiple Elements*/
13    .parent
14    {
15      text-align: center;
16    }
17    /* set the display of child elements*/
18    .child
19    {
20      display: inline-block;
21      text-align: left;
22    }
```

Website design fundamentals and typography

Typography, broadly speaking, affects how text appears to the reader and how the words show up on a page or screen.

We may focus on merely the text we read on websites for our needs. This is because there are many more considerations to take into account when working for the web than there are when writing for print.

In addition to readability, the digital text needs to be created for:

- Shorter attention spans: There are several websites to choose from, many of which have superior lettering.
- Skimmability: Because people often visit websites in search of certain information, they want to get it quickly.
- Because not all internet users view or utilize online content, in the same manner, accessibility is important.
- A variety of screen sizes and device types: Text should be readable on all digital platforms.

Web typography receives its unique category to account for all of these factors.

Web typography also includes the fonts, colors, and style we use to create the text's visual appearance as well as the way we show the text on each web page. These small nuances add up to a comfortable reading experience for as many people as possible, thus they are all important.

Although typography in web design is comparable to that in print design, there are a few things to keep in mind to maintain readability on all sorts of screens. To make reading enjoyable, the typographic elements of typeface, type size, color, line height, and letter forms must all be properly harmonized.

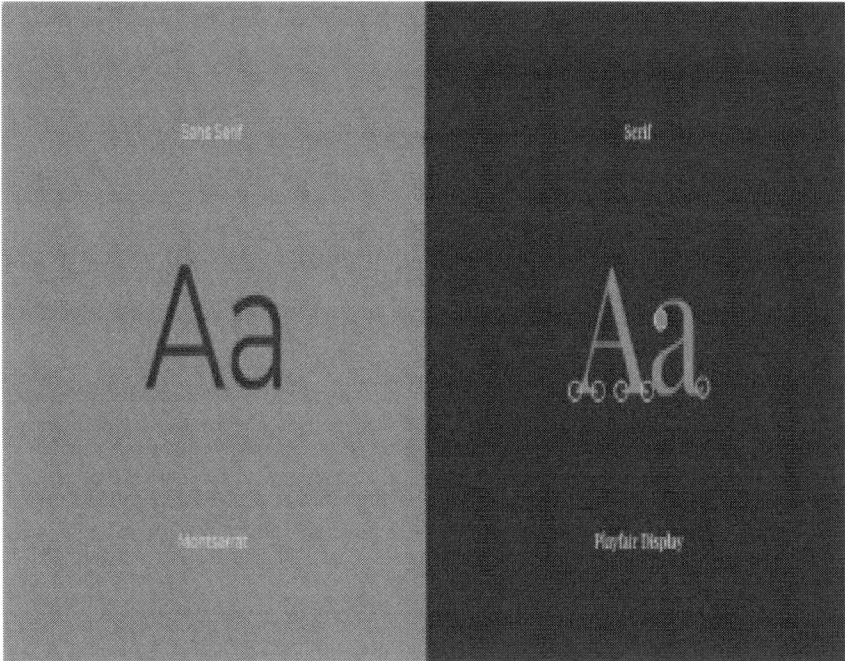

How to use CSS float and clear

The float property is used to format and position content, for as letting an image float to the left of text within a container.

One of the following values may be present for the float property:

- **Left**: The element floats to the left of the element's container.
- **Right**: The element floats to its container's right.
- **None**: The object is not floatable (will be displayed just where it occurs in the text). This is the norm.
- **Inherit**: The element takes on its parent's float value.

See the screenshot below showing the syntax for floating an element.

Add the clear attribute to the element that needs to clear the float. Normally, this comes after the floating element. The left, right, or both can all be values for the clear attribute. You should typically utilize both. The cleared element's neighboring elements and their side restrictions are specified by the CSS clear attribute.

See the screenshot below showing the syntax for clearing an element:

```
File   Edit   Selection   View   Go   Run   Te
<> contact.html  ●        # index2.css  ●
C: > Web Design > web > # index2.css >
1     footer {
2     |    clear: both;
3     }
```

How to combine CSS selectors and understand selector priority

Something that illustrates how the selectors relate to one another is called a combinator. More than one simple selector may be included in a CSS selection. We can sandwich a combinator between the straightforward selectors. There are four different combinators in CSS, they are:

- Descendant selector (space).
- Child selector (>).
- Adjacent sibling selector (+).
- General sibling selector (~).
1. **Descendant Selector**

All elements that are descendants of a given element are matched by the descendant selector. The example that follows selects out every p element contained inside a div element:

```
<> contact.html ●      # index2.css ●

C: > Web Design > web > # index2.css > ...
  1    div p {
  2      background-color: ■yellow;
  3    }
  4    |
```

2. Child Selector (>)

The child selector chooses all elements that are a certain element's children.

The example that follows selects every <p> element that is a div   element's   child:

```
<> contact.html ●      # index2.css ●

C: > Web Design > web > # index2.css > ...
  1    div > p {
  2      background-color: ■yellow;
  3    }
  4
```

3. Adjacent Sibling Selector (+)

The near sibling selector is used to choose an element that follows another particular element exactly. Adjacent indicates "directly after," and siblings' items must have the same parent element.

The first `<p>` element that is positioned right after `<div>` elements is selected in the example below:

```
<> contact.html ●    # index2.css ●
C: > Web Design > web > # index2.css > ...
1    div + p {
2        background-color: ■yellow;
3    }
4    |
```

4. General Sibling Selector (~)

The generic sibling selection chooses every element that is a given element's next sibling. The instance that follows selects all `<p>` elements that are a div element's closest siblings:

```
<> contact.html ●    # index2.css ●
C: > Web Design > web > # index2.css > ...
1    div ~ p {
2        background-color: ■yellow;
3    }
4    |
```

Priority: Using an element ID, such as #some-id-here, is always the best and simplest selection. If only we had such good fortune each time.

Writing selectors should emphasize findings in the following order:

- ID, name, class, or anything else that is unique to the element.
- Complex CSS selectors.
- XPath selectors.

The last resort is to ask a developer to add a special ID or class to the element you are attempting to select if none of the options above work for you.

CHAPTER FOUR

UNDERSTANDING BOOTSTRAP 4

A front-end framework called Bootstrap makes it easier and faster to create mobile-responsive websites. It was initially created by Twitter and is currently used to power everything from websites to WordPress themes. Among other well-known users, are Spotify and LinkedIn. Additionally, the framework is flexible, easy to use, and free.

You may create intricate websites with Bootstrap and modify them to suit your needs. Additionally, it has extra features like carousels, buttons, popups, and more.

Finally, Bootstrap offers several effort-saving shortcuts for building web pages. To design flexible, mobile-first, and browser-compatible web pages, all you need is a fundamental grasp of HTML and CSS. Below are some of the advantages of Bootstrap:

- Your website will appear great on all devices thanks to responsive web design.

- All that is used in responsive web design is HTML and CSS.
- Responsive web design is not a JavaScript application.

Desktops, tablets, and phones are just a few of the various devices that may be used to access websites. No matter the device, your website should be appealing to the eye and simple to navigate.

Web pages should not leave out information to fit smaller devices, but rather adapt their content to fit any device, such as follows:

1. Desktop.
2. Tablet.
3. Phone.

When you use CSS and HTML to resize, conceal, reduce, enlarge, or reposition the content so that it looks nice on any screen, you are already using responsive web design features.

Responsive Web Design Viewport, Responsive Web Design Grid View, Responsive Web Design Media Queries, Responsive Web Design Images, Responsive Web Design Videos, Responsive Web Design Frameworks, and Responsive Web Design Templates should all be explored to build a reliable responsive web design layout.

How to use Balsamiq to mockup and wireframe websites

A Balsamiq mockup is one of the UI/UX designs that developers frequently use to describe their concepts. You undoubtedly hear the phrase "mockup" being tossed about a lot, whether you consider yourself to be a designer or not.

Full-sized design models known as mockups are used for product presentations and other things. They provide a creative means of putting concepts into action. They can be made in a variety of ways. However, if you have the time and abilities, one option is to utilize specialized graphic tools like Balsamiq.

How to Create Mockups with Balsamiq

A software program called Balsamiq mockup is used to design user interfaces for desktop, mobile, and online apps. It is a tool for creating mockups with a highly graphical user interface. The most recent version is Balsamiq Mockup 3, although there have been other releases and improvements throughout the years. Balsamiq Mockup makes it easier to build designs because it offers both sketch and pre-existing pieces.

See the interface below:

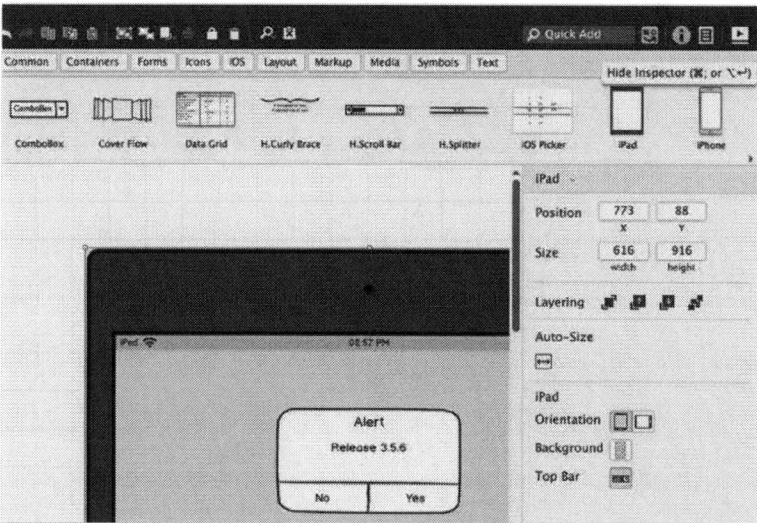

The following are the core benefits of Balsamiq:

- One of Balsamiq's key advantages is that it makes it possible to quickly create wireframes, allowing concepts and ideas to be shared and demonstrated to others without requiring them to fully understand the design's intricacies. The following steps will show you how to build a web application using Balsamiq Mockups:
- By accessing balsamiq.com: There are desktop and online applications. The program also provides a 30-day free trial period after which you must buy a license.
- Creating a mockup: When the program is first used, a blank page is present, allowing the user to upload whatever designs they like. The sign with a + and a red box indicates that you can add more displays.
- The project properties icon is located in the upper right corner of the tool, where you may adjust the project's general characteristics. These include things like descriptions, skin tones, fonts, and colors. The skin, sketch, and wireframe choices that Balsamiq provides are extremely significant icons to remember and utilize before any project is started since it is user-friendly and instructional.
- Designing the screen: There are countless possible elements and combinations, and Balsamiq has prepared templates for each one. Additionally, there are "links" that allow you to access another mockup, or website, or allow you to return to the presentation.
- Mockup saving: You may choose to export a single screen as a PNG image. However, there is an option

to export the project as an interactive clickable wireframe.

The fundamentals of UI design for websites

The goal of user interface (UI) design is to foresee what users would need to accomplish and make sure that the interface contains features that are simple to use, access, and comprehend. Information architecture, interaction design, and graphic design ideas are all incorporated in UI.

Choosing Interface Elements

Try to be consistent and predictable in your choices and their layout since users have become accustomed to specific interface components behaving in a certain way. Task completion, efficiency, and satisfaction everyone will benefit from doing this.

Interface elements include the following but are not limited to:

- **Input Controls**: These are buttons, checkboxes, text fields, checkboxes, radio buttons, list boxes, dropdown lists, list boxes, toggles, and date fields.
- **Navigational Components**: These are search field, breadcrumb, slider, pagination, slider, tags, and icons.
- **Informational Components**: tooltips, message boxes, icons, progress bar, notifications, modal windows.
- **Containers**: Such accordion, etc.

There are instances where using numerous elements to display content may be suitable. When this occurs, it's crucial to take the trade-offs into account. For instance, there are occasions when items that can help you save space instead place greater mental strain on the user by making them guess what is in the dropdown menu or what the element might be.

Best Practices for Designing an Interface

Knowing your users is the foundation for anything; this includes comprehending their objectives, capacities, tastes, and tendencies. When creating your interface after studying more about your user, be sure to take the following factors into account:

- **Maintain an easy-to-use interface:** The best user interfaces are essentially undetectable. They steer away from superfluous parts and utilize straightforward language on labels and in messages.
- **Utilize common UI components to maintain consistency:** Users will feel more at ease and be able to complete tasks more quickly if your UI uses familiar elements. To increase efficiency, it's crucial to establish recurring language, layout, and design themes across the entire website. Once a user has mastered a task, they need to be able to apply it to other areas of the website.

- **Use deliberate page layout:** Structure the page according to relevance while taking into account the spatial relationships between the elements on it. The most crucial pieces of information can be highlighted with careful positioning, which can also improve scalability and readability.
- **Make thoughtful use of texture and color:** Use color, light, contrast, and texture to your advantage to draw attention to or divert it from objects.
- **Create hierarchy and clarity with typography:** Think very carefully about how you employ typography. The text should be presented in a variety of sizes, fonts, and arrangements to improve readability, scalability, and legibility.
- **Ensure that the system informs users of what is happening at all times:** This should include location, activities, status changes, and errors. Your user's annoyance can be decreased by using different UI components to indicate status and, if necessary, the next steps.
- **Consider the defaults:** You can design defaults that ease the user's load by carefully considering and anticipating the goals visitors bring to your site. When it comes to forming design, where you can have the option to have some fields pre-selected or filled out, this becomes more crucial.

How to download Bootstrap

Follow the procedures below to download Bootstrap to your device:

- Go to Google and type Bootstrap. The Bootstrap links will open.

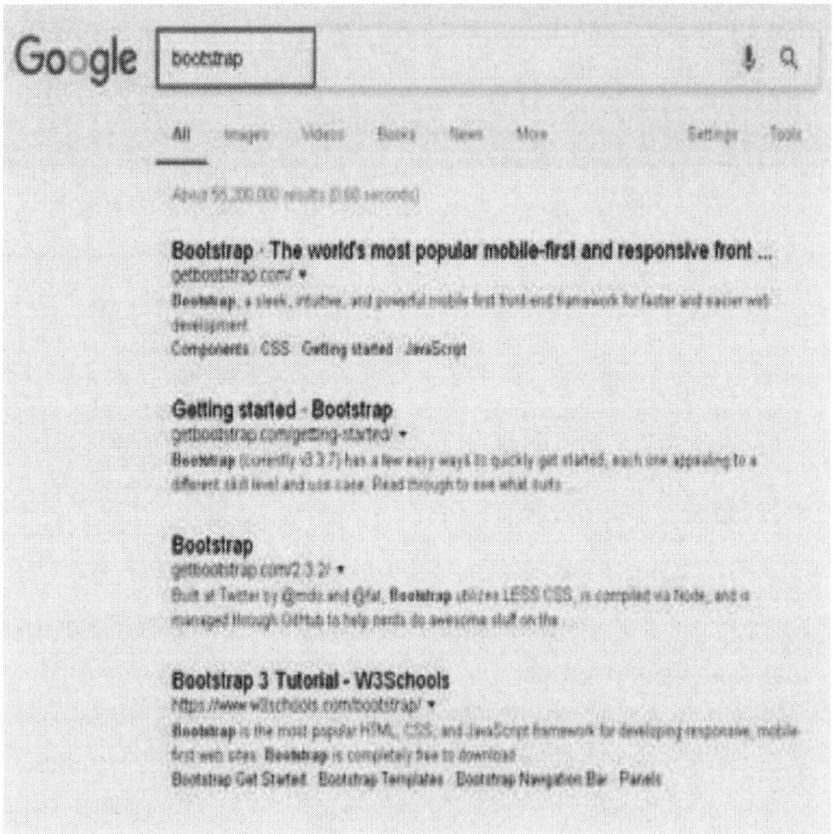

- In the search results, click the first link, which is http://www.getbootstrap.com.

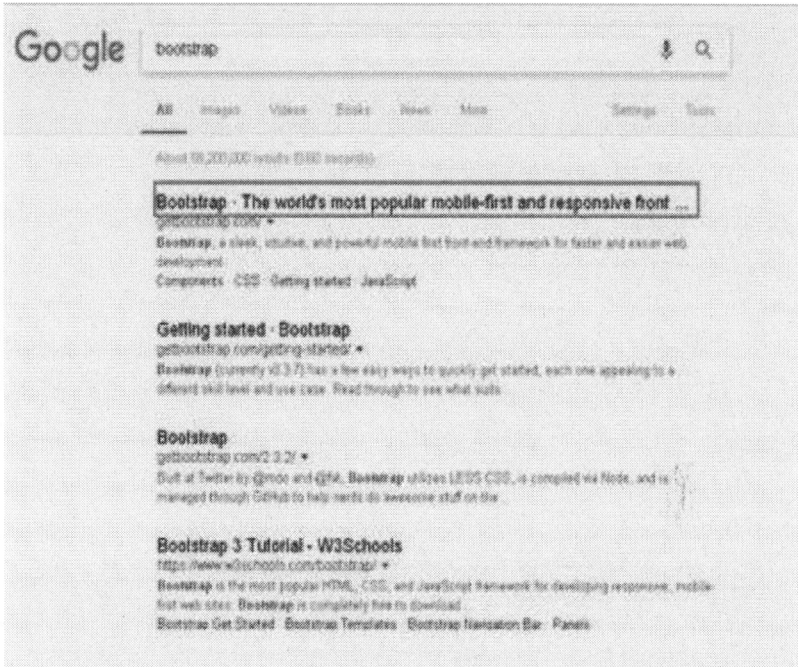

- Select the "Download Bootstrap", but from the page that opens, select the Bootstrap option.

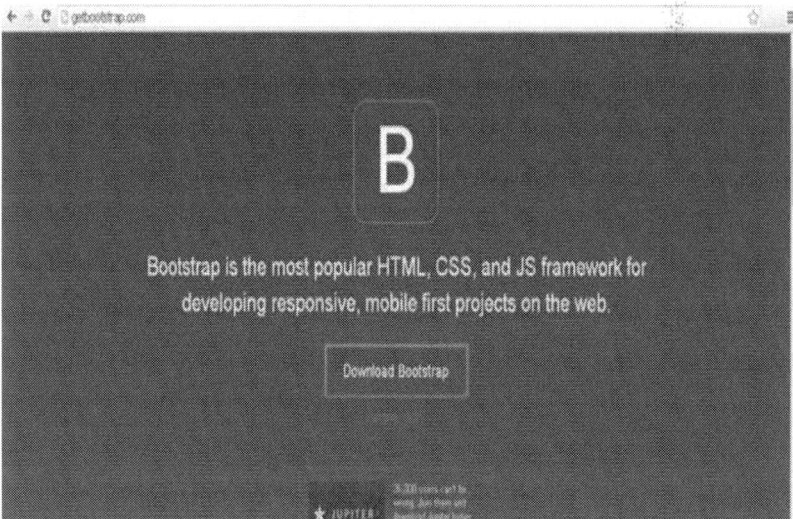

Bootstrap is the most popular HTML, CSS, and JS framework for developing responsive, mobile first projects on the web.

Download Bootstrap

- Extract the files, and move on.
- Three different types of files are available inside the file, (CSS, FONTS, and JS).

Understanding the Bootstrap grid layout system

The layout is handled by the Bootstrap Grid System, especially Responsive Layouts. To understand Bootstrap, you must first grasp how it operates. The Rows and Columns of the Grid are arranged in groups inside one or more Containers. Without Bootstrap JavaScript and other CSS Components, the Bootstrap Grid can be utilized on its own. Only the "bootstrap-grid.css" file, which includes the Grid and Flexbox classes, has to be downloaded and referenced.

Here's the most **basic example** of using the Grid:

```
1   <div class="container">
2     <div class="row">
3       <div class="col">I'm your content inside the grid
4     </div>
5   </div>
```

How to use bootstrap containers to layout your website easily

- The first thing is to create an HTML page.
- Then load Bootstrap via CDN or host it locally.
- After that, Include jQuery.

- Load Bootstrap JavaScript.
- Try to put them together.
- Add a navigation bar.
- Include your custom CSS.
- Create a page content container.
- You should add a background image and custom JavaScript.
- Then add an Overlay.
- Include a page title and body text.
- Create a CTA button.
- Set up a three-column section.
- Add a contact form.
- Include a team section.
- Create a two-column footer.
- Ensure to add media queries.
- Create additional pages.
- Then Create a modal.
- And your website will be live.

Learn to use other Bootstrap components such as buttons

The <button> element is intended to be used in conjunction with the .btn classes. However, these classes can be applied to <a> and <input> components (though some browsers might apply a little different rendering).

Instead of linking to new pages or sections within the current page when using button classes on a> elements that are used to activate in-page features and functions (like collapsing content), such links should indeed be given a role="button" to communicate their function to assistive technologies like screen readers. The various button designs that can be implemented with Bootstrap are listed below.

- .btn
- .btn-default
- .btn-primary
- .btn-success
- .btn-info
- .btn-warning
- .btn-danger
- .btn-link

See the screenshot below showing how to implement different styles of a button using Bootstrap.

```
9     <body>
10
11    <button type="button" class="btn">Basic</button>
12    <button type="button" class="btn btn-default">Default</button>
13    <button type="button" class="btn btn-primary">Primary</button>
14    <button type="button" class="btn btn-success">Success</button>
15    <button type="button" class="btn btn-info">Info</button>
16    <button type="button" class="btn btn-warning">Warning</button>
17    <button type="button" class="btn btn-danger">Danger</button>
18    <button type="button" class="btn btn-link">Link</button>
19
20    </body>
21        </html>
```

Adding symbols using Font Awesome

For use with inline elements, Font Awesome was created. The <i>, and <span> components are frequently employed. Be aware that changing the container's font or color will also change the icon. The same is true for shadow and any other CSS-based inheritance. Add the following to your HTML page's <head> section to use the Font Awesome icons:

<link rel="stylesheet" href="https://cdnjs.cloudflare.com/ajax/libs/font-awesome/4.7.0/css/font-awesome.min.css">

See the screenshot below showing how to implement this.

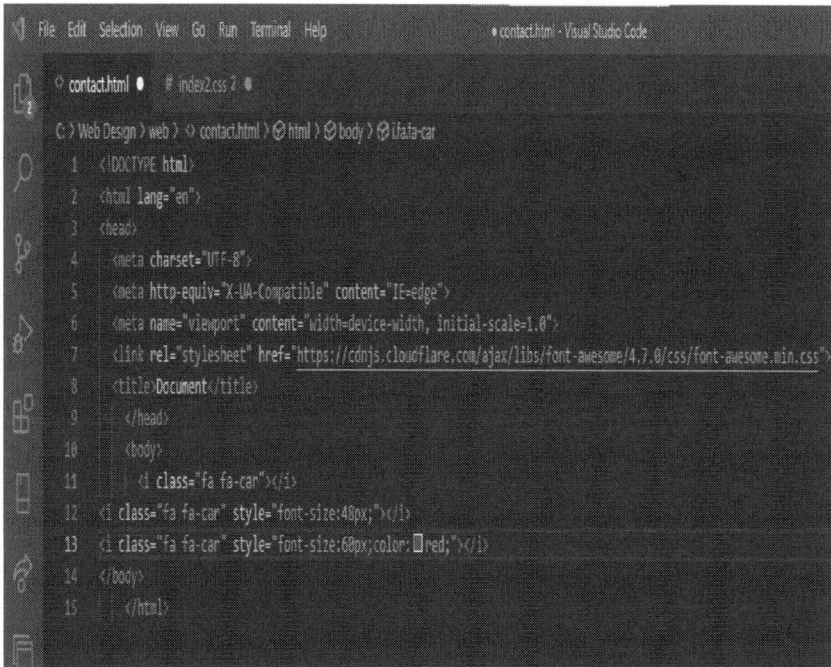

(NB: No downloading or installation is required).

Learn to use Bootstrap carousels

The bootstrap carousel is a slideshow that contains multiple elements. One of the parts of bootstrap is the bootstrap carousel. This is a display that cycles over each item on the screen one at a time. The carousel is a component that saves space and is typically found on websites that sell products. This is one of the sophisticated and animated elements that is utilized to draw users in. Similar to eCommerce websites, the carousel intends to present several items, persons, and components in a single frame. Numerous classes, properties, and tags were utilized by the basic carousel and its control.

See the screenshot below showing how you can implement the Carousels function using Bootstrap.

Learn to add Bootstrap cards to your website

A card is a malleable and expandable content container. It offers options for headers and footers, a variety of content, background colors that are appropriate for the context, and strong display options. Using Bootstrap 3, cards will take the place of our previous panels, wells, and thumbnails. As modifier classes for cards, similar functionality to that of those components are accessible.

Cards are constructed with the least amount of markup and styles possible while yet managing to offer a substantial amount of control and customization. They are easily alignable and blend in with other Bootstrap components thanks to their flexbox construction. Use spacing tools as necessary because they don't come with margins by default.

```
 9 ∨    <body>
10 ∨      <div class="card" style="width: 18rem;">
11          <img src="..." class="card-img-top" alt="...">
12 ∨        <div class="card-body">
13            <h5 class="card-title">Card title</h5>
14            <p class="card-text">Some quick example text to build on the card title and make up the bulk of the card's content.</p>
15            <a href="#" class="btn btn-primary">Go somewhere</a>
16          </div>
17        </div>
18      </body>
19    </html>
```

Using Bootstrap navigation bars

Bootstrap Navbar is a direction-finding header that is situated at the top of the webpage and can be stretched or collapsed, depending on the screen size. Bootstrap Navbar is used **to**

design responsive navigation for the website. Using the <nav class="navbar navbar-default"> tag, we can create a conventional navigation bar. With little effort, we can also make many navbar variations, such as navbars with drop-down menus and search boxes and a fixed navbar. The steps to construct a straightforward static navbar with navigation links are listed below.

```html
    <span class="navbar-toggler-icon"></span>
  </button>
  <div class="collapse navbar-collapse" id="navbarNav">
    <ul class="navbar-nav">
      <li class="nav-item active">
        <a class="nav-link" href="#">Home <span class="sr
      </li>
      <li class="nav-item">
        <a class="nav-link" href="#">Features</a>
      </li>
      <li class="nav-item">
        <a class="nav-link" href="#">Pricing</a>
      </li>
    </ul>
  </div>
</nav>
```

CHAPTER FIVE

JAVASCRIPT

Introduction

One of the most popular programming languages nowadays is JavaScript. It is utilized in game development, desktop apps, mobile applications, client-side web applications, and server-side web applications. It's the ideal moment to learn JavaScript because there is a huge need for JavaScript developers right now. Learning variables, data types, operators, loops, and other concepts will help one get started with JavaScript.

We will discuss the ideas surrounding variables and data types in JavaScript in this blog. You can play around with data and create error-free code by writing it when you are familiar with JavaScript's variables and data types. This blog is the ideal place to start if you are new to JavaScript.

The version of ECMAScript that corresponds to this year is ECMAScript 2022. We could use a few of the new functionalities that have been added to our JavaScript projects.

The new **ECMAScript** features for this year are:

- Top-level await.
- Private instance fields, methods, and accessors.
- Static class fields and methods.

- Static class initialization blocks.
- Error: .cause.
- Array, String, and TypedArray: .at() Method.
- Object: .hasOwn().
- RegExp: match .indices ('d' flag).

The Fundamentals of Code

The fundamental building blocks of all programming languages are the fundamentals. They are the fundamental concepts that every newbie must first comprehend to dive into coding. The foundations of programming remain the same regardless of the programming language you decide to learn. These fundamentals include, among others:

- IDEs and Coding Environments.
- Variable Declaration.
- Basic Syntax.
- Data Type and Structures.
- Flow Control Structures (Conditionals and loops).
- Functional Programming.
- Object-Oriented Programming.
- Debugging.

Applying JavaScript (internal and external)

There are 2 ways to use the javascript in the HTML file:

1. **Internal JavaScript:**

JavaScript code can be embedded directly into the HTML file by writing the code inside a <script> tag. You can add the <script> tag either inside <head> or the <body> tag as you wish.

```
File  Edit  Selection  View  Go  Run  Terminal  Help                    ● contact.html - Visual Studio Code

 ◇ contact.html ●    JS index.js  ●    # index2.css 2 ●

C: > Web Design > web > ◇ contact.html > ⊘ html > ⊘ body > ⊘ script
  1   <!DOCTYPE html>
  2   <html lang="en">
  3   <head>
  4     <meta charset="UTF-8">
  5     <meta http-equiv="X-UA-Compatible" content="IE=edge">
  6     <meta name="viewport" content="width=device-width, initial-scale=1.0">
  7     <link rel="stylesheet" type="text/css" rel="noopener" target="_blank" href="mystyles.css">
  8     <title>JavaScript</title>
  9   </head>
 10   <body>
 11     <h2>Internal JavaScript</h2>
 12     <script>
 13
 14       /*Internal Javascript*/
 15       console.log("Hi Genny, Welcome to GfG");
 16     </script>
 17
 18   </body>
 19   </html>
```

2. External JavaScript:

Another way to do this is to write the JavaScript code in another file with the .js extension, and then link the file **in** the **<head>** or the **<body>** tag of your HTML file where you want to add the code to. External JavaScript is when JavaScript code (script) is written in another file with extension **.js** and then link to your HTML file inside the **< head>** or the **<body>** tag of the HTML file, where the code must be added. Using external JavaScript is more convenient when the same code needs to be used on many different web pages. Using an external script. All you need is just to put the name of the script file, that is the .js file in the src (source) attribute of the **<script>** tag. External **JavaScript** file cannot contain <script> tags.

```
File  Edit  Selection  View  Go  Run  Terminal  Help                        • contact.html - Visual Studio Code

◇ contact.html  •    JS index.js   •    # index2.css 2  •

C > Web Design > web > ◇ contact.html > ⊘ html > ⊘ body
  1    <!DOCTYPE html>
  2    <html lang="en">
  3    <head>
  4        <meta charset="UTF-8">
  5        <meta http-equiv="X-UA-Compatible" content="IE=edge">
  6        <meta name="viewport" content="width=device-width, initial-scale=1.0">
  7        <link rel="stylesheet" type="text/css" rel="noopener" target="_blank" href="mystyles.css">
  8        <title>JavaScript</title>
  9    </head>
 10    <body>
 11        <h2>External JavaScript</h2>
 12        <script src="index.js"></script> /* External Javascript *
 13    </body>
 14    </html>
```

JavaScript attribute values:

- **type:** The JavaScript type is used to state the MIME type of script and identify the content of the Tag. The default value that comes with this attribute is **"text/javascript"**.
- **src:** The src is used to indicate the URL of every external JavaScript file.
- **async:** The async attribute value is a Boolean attribute. When used, it indicates that the script will be executed asynchronously when it's present.

109

- **defer**: This is a Boolean attribute used to indicate that the script is executed as soon as the page has finished parsing.
- **integrity:** This is used to give authorization to the Browser to check the fetched script to make sure that the source code is never loaded.
- **referrer-policy:** This is used to state the reference information that will be forwarded to the server when fetching the script.

Starting code with alerts and prompts

If you want to be sure that the user receives the information, an alert is frequently utilized. The user will need to click "OK" in an alert window to continue. There are three different types of popup boxes available in JavaScript: Alert, Confirm, and Prompt.

Prompts:

If you want the user to enter a value before visiting a page, a prompt is frequently utilized. The user must click "OK" or "Cancel" to continue after providing an input value when a prompt box appears.

The input value is returned to the box if the user hits "OK." but the box returns null when the user hits the "Cancel" button.

The screenshot below shows the syntax.

```html
<!DOCTYPE html>
<html lang="en">
<head>
    <meta charset="UTF-8">
    <meta http-equiv="X-UA-Compatible" content="IE=edge">
    <meta name="viewport" content="width=device-width, initial-scale=1.0">
    <title>Document</title>
</head>
<body>
    <h2>JavaScript Prompt</h2>

<button onclick="myFunction()">Try it</button>

<p id="demo"></p>

<script>
function myFunction() {
  let text;
  let person = prompt("Please enter your name:", "Harry Potter");
  if (person == null || person == "") {
    text = "User cancelled the prompt.";
  } else {
    text = "Hello " + person + "! How are you today?";
  }
  document.getElementById("demo").innerHTML = text;
}
</script>
</body>
</html>
```

Understand Variables and Data Types in JavaScript

An object used to hold data of the types string, integer, Boolean, etc. is a variable. JavaScript is a dynamically or loosely typed language, so the type of data does not need to be specified when declaring a variable. It is capable of determining the data type and changing its behavior when changes are made.

The var keyword was first used to declare variables in JavaScript. Then ES6 introduces let and const. Now that let and const are supported by the majority of browsers, let and const are often used by developers. A variable is declared in a function scope using the var keyword. If a variable is declared inside a function, it can only be accessed from within the function, according to the concept of the function scope. Global access is made available by the global declaration of var. To better understand this, let's see at the program in the screenshot below.

Data types

An attribute of a piece of data called a "data type" dictates how the data must be understood. The eight fundamental data types in JavaScript are Number, BigInt, String, Boolean, null, undefined, Symbol, and Objects. Except for objects, all data types are primitive, which means that the programmer does not need to build them.

Variable naming in JS

A variable is a "named store" for data in JavaScript and other programming languages. It serves as a place to keep values. Variables can be used to hold information about users, visitors, and other things in programs.

The following are the rules that you must follow to create a variable in JavaScript.

- The variable naming rules provide that the initial character of a variable name must be a letter or an underscore (_). A number cannot be the initial character.

- Any letter, any number, or the underscore can be used in the remaining characters of the variable name. Other characters, such as spaces, symbols, and punctuation, are not permitted.

- Variable names adhere to case sensitivity much like the rest of JavaScript. In other words, an interest rate variable is regarded entirely differently from another variable with the same name.

- The variable name can be as long as you want.

- A reserved word in JavaScript cannot be used as a variable name. All programming languages have a set of terms that are used exclusively within the language and cannot be used as variable names due to the potential for misunderstanding (or worse). Also, keep in mind that JavaScript contains a lot of keywords that ought to be avoided.

In the example below, firstName, lastName, cost, tax, and totalPrice are declared variables. And each of them has an item of data stored in them.

```
firstName= "Sam";
lastName= "Dan";
cost= 19.90;
tax= 0.20;
totalPrice = cost + (cost * tax);
```

Working with strings and numbers

Variables in JavaScript can store values of various sorts. But every JavaScript value has a clearly defined type.

Let's start with the differences between strings and numbers in JS.

Strings

Strings in JavaScript are used to store and modify text. A string in JavaScript is defined as zero or more characters enclosed in quotations. In JavaScript, any text enclosed in single or double quote marks is referred to as a string. Simply surround any character construction in quotes to form a string. You need to be aware that quotation marks can be double, single, or backtick.

```
<!DOCTYPE html>
<html>
<body>

<h2>JavaScript Strings</h2>

<p id="demo"></p>

<script>
let text = "John Doe";   // String written inside quotes
document.getElementById("demo").innerHTML = text;
</script>

</body>
</html>
```

Numbers

There is just one kind of number in JavaScript. You can write numbers with or without decimals. In addition to strings, JavaScript variables frequently contain numbers.

Both floating point and integer numbers are possible. JavaScript does not define multiple types of numbers, such

115

as integers, short, long, floating-point, etc., in contrast to many other programming languages.

According to the international IEEE 754 standard, JavaScript numbers are always stored as double precision floating point values. The number (the fraction) is recorded in bits 0 to 51, the exponent in bits 52 to 62, and the sign in bit 63 in the following format, which saves numbers in 64 bits:

See the screenshot below showing how to implement numbers with JavaScript.

```
<!DOCTYPE html>
<html>
<body>

<h2>JavaScript Numbers</h2>

<p>Numbers can be written with or without decimals:</p>

<p id="demo"></p>

<script>
let x = 3.14;
let y = 3;
document.getElementById("demo").innerHTML = x + "<br>" + y;
</script>

</body>
</html>
```

Randomization and logical operators, Loops, and Conditionals

In conditional statements, comparison operators can be used to compare data and do different actions based on the outcome. For instance, if (age < 18) text = "I'm too young to buy alcohol";

see the example below:

```
<!DOCTYPE html>
<html>
<body>

<h2>JavaScript Comparison</h2>

<p>The AND operator (&&) returns true if both expressions are true,
otherwise it returns false.</p>

<p id="demo"></p>

<script>
let x = 6;
let y = 3;

document.getElementById("demo").innerHTML =
(x < 10 && y > 1) + "<br>" +
(x < 10 && y < 1);
</script>

</body>
</html>
```

Logical Operators

To identify the logic between variables or values, logical operators are used. Given that x = 6 and y = 3, the logical operators are explained in the table below:

Operator	Description	Example
&&	and	(x < 10 && y > 1) is true
||	or	(x == 5 || y == 5) is false
!	not	!(x == y) is true

If and only if one or more of its operands are true, the logical OR (||) operator (logical disjunction) for a set of operands is true. It frequently pairs with logical (Boolean) values. It returns a Boolean value if it is. However, when used with non-Boolean values, the || operator will return the value of one of the provided operands, not a Boolean value.

JavaScript Loops

Loops can run a chunk of code repeatedly. If you want to run the same code repeatedly with various values, loops come in handy. When using arrays, this is frequently the case.

```
<!DOCTYPE html>
<html>
<body>

<h2>JavaScript For Loop</h2>

<p id="demo"></p>

<script>
const cars = ["BMW", "Volvo", "Saab", "Ford", "Fiat", "Audi"];

let text = "";
for (let i = 0; i < cars.length; i++) {
  text += cars[i] + "<br>";
}

document.getElementById("demo").innerHTML = text;
</script>

</body>
</html>
```

Different Kinds of Loops

JavaScript provides a variety of loop types,

- for: This repeatedly runs a piece of code.
- for/in: loops through an object's properties.
- for/of: loops through an iterable object's values.
- While: iterates across a block of code as long as a given condition is true.
- do/while: also loops through a block of code while a specified condition is true.

Conditionals

Different actions can be carried out based on different situations using conditional statements. When writing code, you want to take different actions depending on the decision you make rather frequently. When appropriate, conditional statements can be used in your code.

See the screenshot below showing the syntax for conditional statements.

```
<script>
if (condition) {
// block of code to be executed if the condition is true

}
</script>
```

In JavaScript we use conditional statements for the following:

- If you want to tell a block of code to run just if a certain condition is true, use the if statement.
- If the same condition is false, use else to describe a block of code that will be run.
- If the first condition is false, use else if to provide a new condition to test.
- Use switches to define a variety of alternative code blocks to run.

The screenshot below shows how you can implement the "if" conditional statement.

Functions and invocation patterns

A JavaScript function is a section of code created to carry out a certain task. When "something" calls a JavaScript function, it is carried out (calls it). The function keyword is used to define a JavaScript function, which is then followed by the function's name and parenthesis (). Function names may also include underscores, dollar signs, and other characters (same rules as variables). Names of parameters may be included in parenthesis and separated by commas: (parameter1, parameter2, ...). The code that the function will run is enclosed in curly brackets. A **function definition** in JavaScript (also called a **function declaration**, or **function statement**) consists of the function keyword, see the following:

- The name of the function.
- A list of parameters to the function is enclosed in parentheses and separated by commas.
- The JavaScript statements that define the function, enclosed in curly brackets, { /* ... */ }.

The following are the three things you must take note of when dealing with functions:

- The function definition lists the function parameters between parentheses ().
- When a function is called, its parameters are the values that are passed to it.
- The arguments (the parameters) behave as local variables within the function.

See the screenshot below showing how to implement a function in javascript.

```html
<!DOCTYPE html>
<html lang="en">
<head>
    <meta charset="UTF-8">
    <meta http-equiv="X-UA-Compatible" content="IE=edge">
    <meta name="viewport" content="width=device-width, initial-scale=1.0">
    <link rel="stylesheet" type="text/css" rel="noopener" target="_blank" href="mystyles.css">
    <title>Document</title>
</head>
<body>
    <h2>JavaScript Functions</h2>

    <p>This example calls a function which performs a calculation, and returns the result:</p>

    <p id="demo"></p>

    <script>
    function myFunction(p1, p2) {
      return p1 * p2;
    }
    document.getElementById("demo").innerHTML = myFunction(4, 3);
    </script>
</body>
</html>
```

Function Invocation

When "something" invokes (calls) the function, the code inside will run, the following are the conditions under which functions can be invoked.

- When something happens (when a user clicks a button).
- When JavaScript code is used to invoke (call) it.

122

- Automatically (self-invoked).

The example below shows the return of a function when it has been invoked.

```
File  Edit  Selection  View  Go  Run  Terminal  Help          • contact.html - Visual Studio Code

contact.html •    JS index.js  •    # index2.css 2 •

C: > Web Design > web > ◇ contact.html > ⊘ html > ⊘ body > ⊘ script
 1    <!DOCTYPE html>
 2    <html lang="en">
 3    <head>
 4      <meta charset="UTF-8">
 5      <meta http-equiv="X-UA-Compatible" content="IE=edge">
 6      <meta name="viewport" content="width=device-width, initial-scale=1.0">
 7      <link rel="stylesheet" type="text/css" rel="noopener" target="_blank" href="mystyles.css">
 8      <title>Document</title>
 9    </head>
10    <body>
11      <h2>JavaScript Functions</h2>
12
13      <p>This example calls a function which performs a calculation and returns the result:</p>
14
15      <p id="demo"></p>
16
17      <script>
18      var x = myFunction(4, 3);
19      document.getElementById("demo").innerHTML = x;
20
21      function myFunction(a, b) {
22        return a * b;
23      }
24      </script>
25    </body>
26    </html>
```

Discussion of ECMAScript

ECMA (European Computer Manufacturer's Association) is the organization's full name. A standard for scripting languages like JavaScript, JScript, etc. is called ECMAScript. It is a trademarked specification for a scripting language. A language based on ECMAScript is called JavaScript.

ECMAScript is a standard for scripting languages like JavaScript and JScript. One of the most widely used ECMAScript implementations in JavaScript.

The ECMAScript standard is followed by JavaScript. LiveScript was the original name of JavaScript, but Netscape changed it to JavaScript, maybe in response to the buzz that Java was causing. LiveScript, the predecessor to JavaScript, had its debut in Netscape 2.0 in 1995. the language's essential general-purpose functionality that is built into web browsers like Netscape, Internet Explorer, and others.

The most recent revision to the standard in more than four years was ECMAScript Edition 5. The only very slight difference between JavaScript 2.0 and Edition 5 of the ECMAScript standard is that JavaScript 2.0 adheres to Edition 5.

The eighth edition—also referred to as ECMAScript 2017—was made available in June 2017.

The ECMA-262 Specification standardized the base JavaScript language.

Why ECMAScript:

- JavaScript is a lightweight, interpreted programming language.
- Created for the development of network-centric applications.
- Integral and complementary to Java.
- Integral and complementary to HTML.

- Cross-platform and open.

Learn Intermediate JavaScript

Timer, scope control (closures), the keyword "this," events (both with and without jQuery), and object prototypes are examples of intermediate concepts that you should master. We will also go over a few key jQuery ideas related to DOM manipulation and basic animations.

Intermediate JavaScript involves the following:

- **JavaScript Concepts:** Making Use of Developer Tools in Browsers - Timers and intervals (to illustrate dynamism) - Scope management using closures Events, the "this" keyword, and object prototypes are all examples of object-oriented programming in JavaScript.
- **jQuery concept:** Events (you'll find that events may be used both with and without jQuery) - DOM manipulation; - Animations.
- **General Concepts:** Finding the information you need through reading documents. Consider strategies to expand your knowledge of JavaScript as a conclusion.

Learn to use JS Expressions, Operators, Statements, and Declarations

A legitimate set of literals, variables, operators, and expressions make up a JavaScript expression, which evaluates to a single value that is an expression. Depending on the expression, this one value may be a number, a string, or a logical value. An expression is a section of code that produces a result. Any section of code that executes a certain action is called a statement.

An expression is any legal block of code that results in a value when resolved and is composed of a group of literals, variables, operators, and other shorter expressions. A variable name that equals the value we gave it (for example, x = 5) might serve as an expression.

As you likely already know, the value we assign to our variable can be anything from a number to a string, and a Boolean.

There are five primary categories of expression in JavaScript:

- **Arithmetic**: The arithmetic operators such as (+, -, *, /, and %).
- **String:** These expressions take a string of values, such as "nada" or "5.864"
- **Logical**: By using a logical operator like && or ||, these phrases typically equate to true or false.
- **Primary expressions:** These are the fundamental terms and symbols we employ in our JavaScript code, for example: In an execution context, an object's property is referred to via the "this" phrase.
- **Left-hand side expressions:** The left-hand side values that serve as the assignment operator's destination:

Object-Oriented Programming

The idea of classes and objects is central to the programming paradigm known as object-oriented programming (OOP). It is used to organize software into straightforward, reusable classes of code blueprints, which are then utilized to build distinct instances of objects. The object-oriented programming languages JavaScript, C++, Java, and Python are only a few examples.

An example-based programming language is JavaScript. To obtain the properties of other objects, it uses an object as a template. You will discover how JavaScript incorporates object-oriented programming in this article on OOP.

Data is restricted from moving freely throughout the system in object-oriented programming, which sees data as a fundamental component in program development. It prevents unintentional change from an external function and more securely connects data to the function that manipulates it. An issue is divided into several things called objects by OOP, and data and methods are built around these objects.

Object, Class, and Methods are the three principles that make up object-oriented programming. The ES6 JavaScript supports the following Object-Oriented programming components.

- **Object**: The presentation of any entity in real-time is referred to as a real-time object entity.

- **Class**: The blueprint is the first step in the process of building any item that you wish to create.
- **Methods**: The items can communicate with one another.
- **Class inheritance**: Support for class inheritance is provided by ES6. The bravery of inheritance allows it to make new entities out of old ones. In ES6, there are two categories of class:
- **Parent class/superclass**: A parent class or superclass is a class that has been extended to produce a new class.
- **Child/subclasses**: A freshly constructed class is referred to as a child or subclass. Except for the constructor, subclasses inherit all of the attributes from their parent classes.

Benefits of OOP

- OOP presents replicable, straightforward structures for complicated things.
- OOP objects are reusable and transferable between programs.
- Polymorphism enables class-specific behavior.
- Classes frequently contain all relevant information to them, making them easier to debug.
- Secure; encapsulates information to protect it.

Basic concepts of Object-oriented Programming

The concept of Object-oriented Programming is clearly defined under the following elements.

Objects:

In an object-oriented architecture, objects serve as the fundamental run-time bodies. They could stand in for anything that the computer needs to manage, such as a location, a person, an account, a table of data, etc. Additionally, user-defined data such as vectors, times, and lists can be represented as objects. In a program, "customer" and "account" are two objects. The customer object can message for the bank balance.

Classes:

We are aware that objects store both the data and the functions needed to alter it. However, classes can be used to combine the two into a user-defined data type. In a class, any number of objects can be produced. Each object has class data linked with it. Therefore, a class is a grouping of objects of similar types.

Think about the class "Fruits," for instance. Mangos that belong to the class fruit can be created as numerous objects under the class name "Fruit Mango".

Encapsulation:

Data and function are wrapped up or bound into a single entity called a class through encapsulation. The key characteristic of a class is its ability to encapsulate data, making it inaccessible to functions outside of the class and available only to those functions. These operations act as a link between the program and the data of the object.

Inheritance:

Inheritance is the phenomenon where items of one class take on the characteristics of objects of a different class. The idea of hierarchical classification is supported by it. Consider the "car" object, which belongs to the "vehicles" and "lightweight vehicles" classes.

The inheritance principle in OOP ensures reuse. This implies that an existing class can have new features added to it without being changed. Deriving a new class from an existing one is made possible.

Creating Objects in JavaScript

- In JavaScript, the string literal can be used to build an object.
- Making use of the new keyword to create objects.
- Using the object constructor to create an object.

```
File  Edit  Selection  View  Go  Run  Terminal  Help              ● contact.html - Visual Studio Code

◇ contact.html ●    JS index.js  ●    # index2.css 2 ●

C: 〉 Web Design 〉 web 〉 ◇ contact.html 〉 ⊘ html 〉 ⊘ body 〉 ⊘ script 〉 [●] student 〉 ∌ name
 1    <!DOCTYPE html>
 2    <html lang="en">
 3    <head>
 4        <meta charset="UTF-8">
 5        <meta http-equiv="X-UA-Compatible" content="IE=edge">
 6        <meta name="viewport" content="width=device-width, initial-scale=1.0">
 7        <link rel="stylesheet" type="text/css" rel="noopener" target="_blank" href="mystyles.css">
 8        <title>Document</title>
 9        </head>
10        <body>
11            <h2>JavaScript Objects</h2>
12            <script>
13            var student = {
14    name: "Chris",

16    age: 21,
17
18    studies: "Computer Science",
19
20    };
21
22    document.getElementById("demo").innerHTML = student.name + " of the age " + student.age + " studies " + student.studies;
23        </script>
24        </body>
25        </html>
```

Class Implementation in JavaScript

JavaScript uses the ES6 standard to define classes. Consider the following example in the screenshot below.

```
File  Edit  Selection  View  Go  Run  Terminal  Help                                    ● contact.html - Visual Studio Code

◇ contact.html ●    JS index.js    ●    # index2.css 2  ●

C > Web Design > web > ◇ contact.html > ⊘ html > ⊘ body > ⊘ script
    1    <!DOCTYPE html>
    2    <html lang="en">
    3    <head>
    4      <meta charset="UTF-8">                              .
    5      <meta http-equiv="X-UA-Compatible" content="IE=edge">
    6      <meta name="viewport" content="width=device-width, initial-scale=1.0">
    7      <link rel="stylesheet" type="text/css" rel="noopener" target="_blank" href="mystyles.css">
    8      <title>Document</title>
    9      </head>
    10     <body>
    11       <h2>JavaScript Objects</h2>
    12       <script>
    13       class Cars {
    14     constructor(name, maker, price) {
    15      this.name = name;
    16      this.maker = maker;
    17      this.price = price;
    18     }
    19     getDetails(){
    20        return (`The name of the car is ${this.name}.`)
    21     }
    22     }
    23     let car1 = new Cars('Rolls Royce Ghost', 'Rolls Royce', '$315K');
    24     let car2 = new Cars('Mercedes AMG One', 'Mercedes', '$2700K');
    25     console.log(car1.name);
    26     console.log(car2.maker);    |
    27     console.log(car1.getDetails());
    28        </script>
    29     </body>
    30     </html>
```

JS Objects and Prototypes

An object in JavaScript is a separate entity having properties
and a type. Consider comparing it to a cup. A cup is an item
with characteristics. A cup has a design, weight, color,
material, and other characteristics. Similarly, JavaScript
objects can have properties that specify their attributes.

132

A JavaScript object has corresponding attributes. A variable that is connected to an object can be used to describe its property. The only real difference between object properties and regular JavaScript variables is the relationship to objects. The qualities of an object are determined by its properties. You can access an object's properties using a straightforward dot-notation:

See the screenshot below showing how you can implement an object in JavaScript.

```
contact.html    JS index.js    # index2.css 2

C: > Web De:
                The meta element represents various kinds of metadata that cannot be
  1    <!D      expressed using the title, base, link, style, and script elements.
  2    <ht
  3    <he  MDN Reference
  4      <meta charset="UTF-8">
  5      <meta http-equiv="X-UA-Compatible" content="IE=edge">
  6      <meta name="viewport" content="width=device-width, initial-scale=1.0">
  7      <link rel="stylesheet" type="text/css" rel="noopener" target="_blank" href="mystyles.css">
  8      <title>Document</title>
  9      </head>
 10      <body>
 11        <h2>JavaScript Object Literal</h2>
 12        <script>
 13      const myObject = {
 14      city: 'Madrid',
 15      greet() {
 16        console.log(`Greetings from ${this.city}`);
 17      }
 18    }
 19
 20    myObject.greet(); // Greetings from Madrid
 21        </script>
 22      </body>
 23      </html>
```

JavaScript objects can inherit features from one another through prototypes. In this article, we define prototypes, describe prototype chains, and describe how to establish a prototype for an object.

The prototype is a built-in attribute that every JavaScript object has. The prototype chain, which forms because the prototype is an object in and of itself, will have a prototype of its own. When we get to a prototype that contains null for its prototype, the chain comes to an end.

(NB: Prototype is not the name of the attribute of an object that points to it. Although its name is not common, all browsers use prototypes. The Object.getPrototypeOf() method is the usual way to retrieve an object's prototype.)

The code in the screenshot below creates a Date object, then marches up the prototype chain, sorting the prototypes. It indicates that the prototype of myDate is a Date.prototype object and the prototype of that is Object.prototype).

```
const myDate = new Date();
let object = myDate;

do {
  object = Object.getPrototypeOf(object);
  console.log(object);
} while (object);

// Date.prototype
// Object { }
// null
```

This', Scope and Closures

The term "scope" describes the area of a program that allows us to access a variable. Variables specified in outer scopes can be accessed from all inner scopes because of JavaScript's ability to nest scopes. The scope of a variable can be global, module, or block. "While"

Closure consists of a function that has been packaged (contained) with references to the lexical context and its surrounding state. In other words, a closure enables inner functions to access the scope of an outside function. Closures are formed whenever a function is created in JavaScript, during function creation time. A function that has references to the variables in its outer scope is said to be closed. Even though the outside variables are beyond the scope of the function, closures enable this.

There are many uses of closures, from creating class-like structures that store state and implement private methods to passing call-backs to event handlers.

In the screenshot below, init() creates a local variable called name and a function called displayName(). The displayName() function is an inner function that is defined inside init() and is available only within the body of the init() function. Note that the displayName() function has no local variables of its own. However, since inner functions have access to the variables of outer functions, displayName() can access the variable name declared in the parent function, init().

```
function init() {
  var name = 'Mozilla'; // name is a local variable created by init
  function displayName() {
    // displayName() is the inner function, a closure
    console.log(name); // use variable declared in the parent function
  }
  displayName();
}
init();
```

Refactoring and Debugging

Refactoring involves reorganizing code without modifying its original functionality. Refactoring is the process of making numerous small changes to code without changing how it behaves externally.

Refactoring is the process of updating a piece of code without affecting how it functions in JavaScript and other languages as well. In other words, you can fiddle with a function, class, module, and so on, and internal structure without affecting the output it generates.

Refactoring became more commonplace with the emergence of agile approaches. For instance, refactoring is a crucial but frequently skipped phase of the test-driven development process.

Refactoring is crucial since it improves the quality of your code. Refactoring frequently keeps your code maintainable, simple to read and navigate, and duplicate-free. Refactoring makes your code easier to read and maintain, which reduces the likelihood that you or other developers will introduce issues. But even if some faults do manage to slip through, it will be simpler to find and fix them.

Refactoring is frequently thought of as a remedy for code smells, which are indications that a codebase may have more serious issues.

Below are the three (3) JavaScript Refactoring Techniques for Clean Code:

1. **Extract Function**: By removing a component of a function's code, it is possible to better describe what that section of code performs. We already no longer have control over that section of the code when we add numerous responsibilities to a single function.
2. **Describe the parameter object**: When handling data in a program, it's common for some of them to be utilized collectively in numerous functions and for various goals. The relationship between the data pieces can be seen when they are organized into a structure, such as an object. The flexibility this refactoring gives a function, though, is its true advantage.
3. **Combine Functions into a Class:** When using a group of actions operating on a common entity, using a class makes more explicit what common environment these methods will share. It makes more readable code and encapsulates together functionalities by their behavior.

Debugging

Logic or syntax problems can occur in programming code. Many of these mistakes are challenging to diagnose. Errors in programming code frequently result in nothing happening. You won't receive any error notifications or directions on where to look for them. Code debugging is the process of looking for (and fixing) mistakes in programming code.

JavaScript Debuggers

Debugging is difficult. But happily, there is a JavaScript debugger included in every current browser. Errors must be notified to the user by default because built-in debuggers can be turned on and off. A debugger also allows you to set breakpoints (points at which code execution can be halted) and look at variables while the code is running.

Normally, press the F12 key to enable debugging in your browser, then choose "Console" from the debugger menu, or else follow the instructions at the bottom of this page. If your browser allows for debugging, you can display JavaScript values in the debugger window by using the console.log() method as follows: View the screenshot below to see how to put this into practice.

```
<title>JavaScript</title>
</head>
<body>
    <p>Activate debugging in your browser (Chrome, IE, Firefox) with F12, and select "Console" in the debugger menu.</p>

    <script>
    a = 5;
    b = 6;
    c = a + b;
    console.log(c);
    </script>

</body>
</html>
```

CHAPTER SIX

DOCUMENT OBJECT MODEL (DOM)

Learn the tree structure of HTML-based websites.

The architecture of a typical HTML (Hypertext Markup Language) or DHTML (Dynamic Hypertext Markup Language) web script is called a Document Object Model, or DOM for short. DOM is essentially a tree with numerous branches and sub-branch levels that describe various webpage elements. The tree's branches stand in for several elements. In the DOM structure, each element may be referred to as a single node. If an HTML element has one or more attributes, the branch will split into different nodes depending on how many attributes the element has. The number of characteristics on an HTML page affects how many nodes form.

The representation of DOM uses a hierarchical tree structure. The document node is the initial node in the DOM. This is so because the HTML page's whole web code is just a document. The root node is the tag, and all of the child nodes are those that are physically connected to the root node.

DOM is an application programming interface that serves as a structural representation of web pages rather than a language (API). The Inspect Element tool in web browsers is one of the typical ways to access the DOM. Making necessary temporary adjustments to the web pages is made easier by using the console tool in the inspect element. HTML and CSS files may have changed as a result. For instance, using the console tool, we may access the <head> portion of the current HTML page by entering console.log(document.head).

See below the tree structure of DOM:

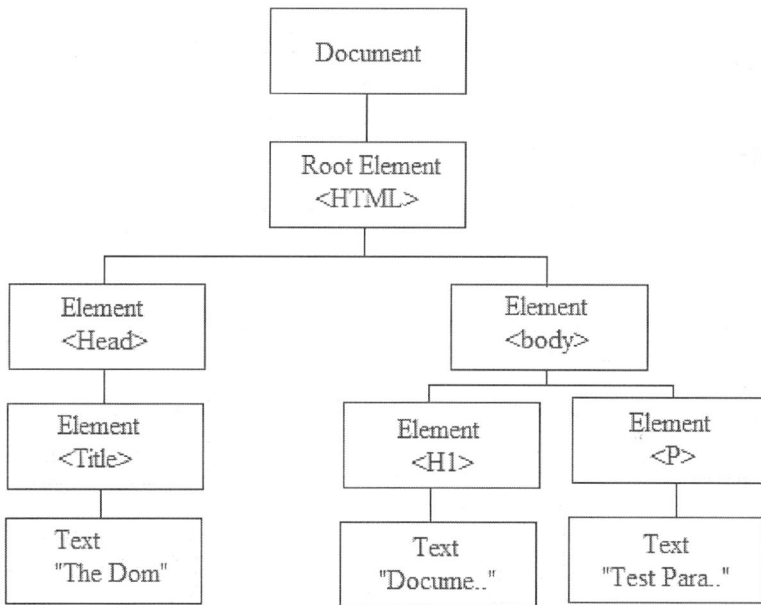

Nodes are the definition of all objects in the DOM. There are many other kinds of nodes, but the three that we use the most frequently are as follows:

- Text nodes.
- Element nodes.
- Comment nodes.

Let's take a look at this simple example:

```
File Edit Selection View Go Run Terminal Help                    • contact.html - Visual Studio Code

contact.html •    JS index.js •    # index2.css 2 •

C: > Web Design > web > <> contact.html > ⊘ html > ⊘ head > ⊘ title
  1   <!DOCTYPE html>
  2   <html lang="en">
  3   <head>
  4       <meta charset="UTF-8">
  5       <meta http-equiv="X-UA-Compatible" content="IE=edge">
  6       <meta name="viewport" content="width=device-width, initial-scale=1.0">
  7       <link rel="stylesheet" type="text/css" rel="noopener" target="_blank" href="mystyles.css">
  8       <title>Simple HTML Document</title>
  9   </head>
 10   <body>
 11       <h2>Internal JavaScript</h2>
 12       <script>
 13       /*Internal Javascript*/
 14       console.log("Hi Genny, Welcome to GfG");
 15       </script>
 16
 17   </body>
 18   </html>
```

Traverse through the document using object notation

To explore, find, or alter elements and/or content within an XML/HTML document, the DOM's elements are arranged into a tree-like data structure.

To "discover" HTML elements (DOM Nodes) based on their relationships to other elements, developers "travel through"

141

the DOM. Start with one option and work your way through it until you find the desired elements.

Every node in the DOM has the document object as its root. Similar to how you may depict your lineage as a "family tree," DOM portrays an HTML page as a tree. Understanding how to deal with JavaScript and HTML requires learning how to go from branch to branch and up and down the DOM tree. The document object is the root object in a tree structure, and depending on where it is in the tree structure, it may have parents, children, and siblings. A Node is a name given to each component of a tree structure.

Each node in the DOM tree is an object that represents a specific page element. Nodes have a lot of information about themselves and are aware of their connections to other nodes in their surrounding area. The node closest to the document in the DOM hierarchy or one level above it is considered a node's parent. A node's children are the nodes one level behind it. Any node on the same tree level in the DOM is a node's sibling. Except for childNodes, every property contains a reference to another node object. There is a reference to an array of nodes in the childNodes attribute. There are several standard methods one can use to select one or more nodes from an HTML document. The three most popular are:

- getElementById.
- getElementsByClassName.
- getElementsByTagName.

See the screenshot below showing how to implement traverse in the document using object notation.

```
File  Edit  Selection  View  Go  Run  Terminal  Help                        • contact.html - Visual Studio Code

◇ contact.html  •     JS index.js   •    # index2.css  •

C: > Web Design > web > ◇ contact.html
  1      <!DOCTYPE html>
  2      <html lang="en">
  3  ∨   <head>
  4        <meta charset="UTF-8">
  5        <meta http-equiv="X-UA-Compatible" content="IE=edge">
  6        <meta name="viewport" content="width=device-width, initial-scale=1.0">
  7        <link rel="stylesheet" type="text/css" rel="noopener" target="_blank" href="mystyles.css">
  8  ∨     <title>Simple HTML Document</title>
  9        </head>
 10  ∨   <body>
 11          <p>Days:</p>
 12  ∨       <ul id="days">
 13            <li id="col1">Sunday</li>
 14            <li id="col2">Monday</li>
 15            <li id="col3">Tuesday</li>
 16            <li id="col3">Wednesday</li>
 17          </ul>
 18          <button onclick="findDay()">Try it</button>
 19  ∨       <script>
 20  ∨         function findDay() {
 21              var fChild = document.getElementById("days").childNodes[1].innerHTML;
 22              alert("First Child :" + fChild);
 23            }
 24          </script>
 25        </body>
 26      </html>
```

Separation of concerns and coding best practices

Programmers utilize the separation of concerns approaches to divide an application into manageable pieces with little overlap in their respective functions. Utilizing software layers,

143

encapsulation, and modularization, the separation of concerns is accomplished.

Separation of Concerns is a guiding idea in development. According to this approach, software should be divided according to the kind of tasks it handles. Consider a program that, among other things, uses logic to determine which objects are important enough to display to the user and formats them in a specific way to make them stand out. The behavior that determines which items to format should be kept apart from the behavior that formats the items since these behaviors are distinct issues that are only incidentally connected.

By logically isolating the main business behavior from the infrastructure and user-interface logic in an architectural manner, programs can be logically constructed to adhere to this notion. Business logic and rules should ideally be contained in a separate project that is independent of other projects in the application. The business model may be tested easily and can change without being firmly tied to low-level implementation details because of this separation (it also helps if infrastructure concerns depend on abstractions defined in the business layer). One important factor driving the adoption of layers is the separation of concerns.

Coding best practices

Multiple DOM activities are carried out when creating a dynamic web application (e.g., adding a new element, updating the style of an element, or removing an element).

We can retain some coding standards when doing such a DOM activity without compromising the speed of our web application.

1. Utilize the Class or ID selector

Use the class or id of the element rather than a standard selector when looking up an element from the DOM (like element name).

2. Use query parent rather than document

If the parent element is already cached when you search an element in the DOM, search in the parent element rather than the document.

3. Use a fragment rather than attaching elements directly

Use a fragment and then append it to the DOM when dynamically adding new elements rather than doing so straight to the DOM node.

4. Instead of adding style directly, use a class with a predefined style

Imagine that you need to modify the ul's background and text colors when the cursor hovers over them. In this case, you would use the style definition included in the CSS file.

Manipulate and change the HTML elements using your understanding of the DOM

145

A single element's ID is the quickest way to find it in the DOM. The document object's getElementById() method allows you to retrieve an element by ID. Get the element and assign it to the demold variable in the console. Our complete HTML element will be returned if demold is logged to the console.

1. To begin any DOM modification, you must first have access to the document object.

2. The HTML root element, a subclass of the document object, comes next.

3. The body and head elements, which are cousins and descendants of the HTML element, are listed next.

4. Below the head element is the title element, which you can probably agree is the parent of the text node "my text" and a child of the head element.

5. The two components (a tag and an h1 tag) that are immediately below the body element are siblings and are also offspring of the body element.

6. The tag's last two children are the href attribute and the text node "my link." The text node "My header" is a child of the h1 element in the same way.

See the screenshot below showing how to implement DOM using getElementById() and getElementByClassName() and other element.

```
contact.html ●    JS index.js    ●    # index2.css 2 ●

C: > Web Design > web > <> contact.html > ⊘ html > ⊘ body > ⊘ script
  1    <!DOCTYPE html>
  2    <html lang="en">
  3    <head>
  4      <meta charset="UTF-8">
  5      <meta http-equiv="X-UA-Compatible" content="IE=edge">
  6      <meta name="viewport" content="width=device-width, initial-scale=1.0">
  7      <link rel="stylesheet" type="text/css" rel="noopener" target="_blank" href="mystyles.css">
  8      <title>Simple HTML Document</title>
  9      </head>
 10      <body>
 11        <p class="master2">i love javascript</p>
 12        <p class="master2">i love react</p>
 13        <h1 class="master2">i want a job</h1>
 14
 15        <button id="btn">click me</button>
 16
 17    <script>
 18
 19    const btn = document.getElementById('btn')
 20
 21        btn.addEventListener('click', function master(){
 22            var master = document.getElementsByClassName("master2");
 23            master[2].innerHTML = 'i need a job';
 24        })
 25
 26    </script>
 27      </body>
 28      </html>
```

147

CHAPTER SEVEN

JQUERY

Understanding jQuery

John Resig developed the quick and concise jQuery JavaScript library in 2006 with the catchphrase "Write less, accomplish more." For quick web development, jQuery makes navigating HTML documents, event handling, animation, and Ajax interactions simpler.

An open-source library for minifying JavaScript called jQuery was developed to make JavaScript operations easier. When compared to using HTML code, jQuery allows you to swiftly code a variety of different instructions.

jQuery is a JavaScript library for independent platforms that were created to facilitate HTML client-side scripting. One of the most well-known Java script libraries now in use is jQuery. It is known that 65 percent of the top one million company websites on the internet have it installed. It is free and open-source (FOSS) software that is authorized under the MIT license.

For the development of dynamic websites and web apps, jQuery is employed. The building of applications is made easier by the abundance of jQuery plugins.

JQuery's syntax is created in a way that makes it simple to utilize for document navigation. It grants developers the ability to create plugins for the JavaScript library. Additionally, it helps the developers create an abstraction for animation, widgets with custom themes, and worse interactivity. In general, jQuery statements begin with a dollar sign ($) and end with a semicolon (;).

The dollar sign ($) in jQuery is merely a shortcut for jQuery. Let's have a look at the example code below, which shows the most fundamental jQuery statement.

Basic syntax is: $(selector).action(), and are explained below:

- A $ sign to define/access jQuery.
- A (selector) to "query (or find)" HTML elements.
- A jQuery action() to be performed on the element(s).
- Examples of jQuery functions:
- $(this).hide() - hides the current element.
- $("p").hide() - hides all <p> elements.
- $(".test").hide() - hides all elements with class="test".
- $("#test").hide() - hides the element with id="test".

jQuery Features

By writing less code, jQuery makes many programming tasks easier. The list of significant core features that jQuery supports is provided below.

- **DOM manipulation**: Using Sizzle, a cross-browser open source selection engine, jQuery makes it simple to choose DOM elements, negotiate with them, and modify their content.

- **Event handling**: Using jQuery eliminates the need to clog up the HTML code with event handlers to elegantly capture a range of occurrences, such as a user clicking a link.

- **AJAX Support**: Using AJAX technology, jQuery greatly facilitates the development of a responsive and feature-rich website.

- **Animations**: You can employ a variety of jQuery's built-in animation effects on your websites.

- **Small size**: The jQuery library is only roughly 19KB in size (Minified and gzipped).

- **Cross-Browser Support**: jQuery is cross-browser compatible and performs well with IE 6.0 and later, Firefox 2.0 and later, Safari 3.0 and later, Chrome, and Opera 9.0 and later.

- **Up-to-date technology**: jQuery supports XPath syntax basics and CSS3 selectors.

Installing and using the jQuery

Before you can begin to install and use jQuery, you just need to download it into your device.

There are two versions of jQuery available for downloading:

- Production version: This is the version of your live website that has been compressed and minified.

- Test and development versions are available here (uncompressed and readable code).

From jQuery.com, both versions can be downloaded.

The jQuery library is usually a single JavaScript file, and you reference it with the HTML <script> tag. Note that the <script> tag should be inside the <head> section.

See the screenshot below.

```html
∨ <head>
    <meta charset="UTF-8">
    <meta http-equiv="X-UA-Compatible" content="IE=edge">
    <meta name="viewport" content="width=device-width, initial-scale=1.0">
    <link rel="stylesheet" type="text/css" rel="noopener" target="_blank" href="mystyles.css">
    <script src="jquery-3.6.0.min.js"></script>
    <title>Simple HTML Document</title>
  </head>
```

- Go to your web browser and type https://jQuery.com on the address bar and press enter key on your keyboard.
- Click on the downloadable file.
- Copy the js file into your root web directory eg. www.test.com/jquery-3.6.0.min.js.
- Then add index.php or index.html between the head tags include the following code, <script type="text/javascript" src="jquery-3.6.0.min.js"></script> or <script src="https://ajax.googleapis.com/ajax/libs/jquery/3.6.0/jquery.min.js"></script> for CDN, and then JQuery will be installed.

151

Why learn jQuery?

You may create visually appealing static web pages using HTML and CSS. These static websites can have dynamic functionality added to them with a little help from JavaScript. With the help of the JavaScript library jQuery, you can add a variety of dynamic behavior to layouts that would otherwise lack creativity.

Learning about jQuery functionality

JQuery's functionality explains how it works. These are features that users can incorporate into their programs. You can use jQuery to implement the following essential features.

1. Regular JavaScript Functions

Using a function declaration is the first and most straightforward technique to declare a function in JavaScript. The following syntax can be used to construct the multiply() function, which accepts the two parameters x and y, multiplies them, and returns the result:

```
function multiply(x,y) {
    return x * y;
}
console.log( multiply(2, 2) );
```

The current scope is topped by functions defined in this manner (a function declaration). The function might be put before the console.log() and still function.

2. JavaScript Function Expressions

It is possible to express the same function as an expression that consciously sets a variable.

```javascript
const multiply = function(x,y) {
    return x * y;
}

console.log( multiply(2, 2) );
```

The function can only be used after it has been defined because it is not hoisted.

3. Object Literal Method Definitions

You can define a function in another object since in JavaScript they are treated the same as any other value type. For example:

```javascript
const mathLib = {

// property
PI: 3.14,

// multiply(x,y) method
multiply: function(x, y) {
    return x * y;
},

// divide(x,y) method
divide: function(x, y) {
    return x / y;
}

}

console.log( mathLib.multiply(2, 2) );
```

Again, this object method can only be called after it has been defined.

4. ES2015 Arrow Functions

Arrow functions can only be assigned to a variable or used anonymously; they don't need the function keyword (such as in a callback or event handler). A function is indicated in the following code block by an arrow (=>) after a parameter surrounded in rounded brackets (()):

```
const multiply = (x, y) => { return x * y; };

console.log( multiply(2, 2) );
```

Since there is only one statement, the return is implied and the brackets are unnecessary for functionality that is the same but requires a simpler syntax:

```
const multiply = (x, y) => x * y;
```

Those brackets may also be dropped when the function only takes one parameter:

```
const square = x => x ** 2;
```

Even though there is still one parameter for which brackets are needed:

```
const estimatePI = () => 22 / 7;
```

There is no need to use .bind(this) because arrow functions automatically assign this to the value in the immediate outer scope.

5. jQuery Extension Functions

Making functions is very similar because the jQuery extension function is a JavaScript library. However, you can increase jQuery's functionality by including your unique methods. The jQuery prototype ($.fn) object is extended via the jQuery.fn.extend() method to enable chaining of new functionality to the primary jQuery() function.

For example, the following code defines new check and uncheck jQuery methods to modify checkbox input fields:

```javascript
jQuery.fn.extend({

// check checkboxes
check: function() {
    return this.each(function() {
        this.checked = true;
    });
},

// uncheck checkboxes
uncheck: function() {
    return this.each(function() {
        this.checked = false;
    });
}

});

// check all checkboxes on the page
$( "input[type='checkbox']" ).check();
```

6. Keeping it Functional

Although function syntax is frequently a matter of taste, try to keep your code legible. Using a function statement might be preferable to confusing oneself later on with a creative but unintelligible jumble of arrows and brackets.

Differences between jQuery and Angular JavaScript

jQuery is a JavaScript library that is open-source and free and used for web page client-side development. To reduce the number of lines of code and make JavaScript more interactive and dynamic, its developers created it in 2006 and released it under the MIT License.

A highly well-liked library among JavaScript programmers is jQuery. Whether it's Amazon, Zoom, or Quora. Research shows that more than 77.9% of all websites on the internet employ jQuery, this is according to W3techs. "While",

AngularJS is a Typescript-based web framework used to build the front end of scalable, and cross-platform web applications. It offers certain essential features, including dependency injection, directives, two-way data flow, and unit testing.

Global leaders in Angular usage include Google, PayPal, and Forbes. Because of its scalability, fast performance, and user-friendly data binding, Angular JS is recommended as a front-end framework by many companies, however, jQuery is more popular.

Introduction to functions in jQuery

The syntax for defining a function in jQuery is entirely different from that in JavaScript. A function is a collection of statements that accept input, carry out a certain calculation, and output the results. A function is essentially a group of statements that execute a particular operation or do a calculation and then return the result to the user.

The goal is to group similar or often performed actions into a function so that we may call it rather than writing the same code again for various inputs.

See the screenshot of the syntax below:

```
$.fn.myFunction = function(){}
```

The example in the screenshot below shows how you can implement the jQuery function in your program as shown in the screenshot below.

```
<title>Simple HTML Document</title>
<script src=
"https://code.jquery.com/jquery-1.12.4.min.js">
    </script>
    <script>
        $(document).ready(function() {
            $.fn.myFunction = function() {
                document.getElementById("geeks").innerHTML
                    = "JQuery function is defined!";
            }

            $(".gfg").click(function(){
                $.fn.myFunction();
            });
        });
    </script>
</head>
<body style="text-align:center">

    <h1 style="color:□green;">
        GeeksforGeeks
    </h1>

    <h3>
        Defining function in jQuery
    </h3>

    <p id="geeks"></p>

    <button type="button" class="gfg">
        Click
    </button>
</body>
</html>
```

Manipulating text, styles, and attributes with jQuery

The following screenshot lists jQuery methods to get or set the value of an attribute, property, text, or HTML.

jQuery Method	Description
attr()	Get or set the value of specified attribute of the target element(s).
prop()	Get or set the value of specified property of the target element(s).
html()	Get or set html content to the specified target element(s).
text()	Get or set text for the specified target element(s).
val()	Get or set value property of the specified target element.

158

The following screenshot shows various jQuery methods to access the DOM element's attributes, properties, and values. Study the screenshot carefully.

```
$('#myDiv').attr('class')    $('#myDiv').prop('class')

<div id="myDiv" class="divCls">                          $('#myDiv').html()
    <p style="background-color:yellow;width:100%">
        This is paragraph.                               $('#myDiv').text()
    </p>
</div>                                           $('input:text').val()
<div id="firstNameDiv">
    <label>First Name</label><input type="text" value="John" />
</div>
<input type="button" value="Get Value" id="addBtn" style="width: 100px" />

    $('label').text()       $('input:button').val()

                         $('input:button').prop('style').width
```

See the screenshot below showing how you can manipulate text, styles, and attributes with jQuery using the jQuery attr() Method.

159

```
contact.html  ●    JS  index.js    ●   # index2.css 2  ●

> Web Design > web > <> contact.html > ⊘ html > ⊘ body > ⊘ p
9       <script src="https://ajax.googleapis.com/ajax/libs/jquery/1.11.2/jquery.min.js">
10      </script>
11      <script>
12        $(document).ready(function () {
13          $('#btnDivStyle').click(function(){
14            alert($('div').attr('class'));
15          });
16          $('#btnPStyle').click(function(){
17            alert($('p').attr('style'));
18          });
19          $('div').attr('class','yellowDiv');  // adds class='yellowDiv' to each div element
20        });
21      </script>
22      <style>
23        .yellowDiv{
24          background-color: ▪yellow;}
25      </style>
26      </head>
27      <body>
28        <h1>Demo: jQuery attr() method</h1>
29        <button id="btnDivStyle">Get div class</button>
30        <button id="btnPStyle">Get p Style</button> </br></br>
31        <div>
32          This is div.
33        </div>
34        <p style="font-size:16px;font-weight:bold">
35          This is paragraph. </p>
36        <div>
37          This is div.
38        </div>
39        <p style="color: ▪red">
40          This is paragraph.
41        </p>
42      </body>
```

The first <p> element in an HTML page's style attribute is obtained in the example above by calling $('p').attr('style'). Not all of the <p> elements' style properties are returned.

See the screenshot below showing how you can manipulate text, styles, and attributes with jQuery using **the** jQuery html() Method.

160

```
<> contact.html ●      JS index.js    ●    # index2.css 2 ●

C: > Web Design > web > <> contact.html > ⊘ html > ⊘ body > ⊘ div#emptyDiv
    8       <title>Simple HTML Document</title>
    9       <script src="https://ajax.googleapis.com/ajax/libs/jquery/1.11.2/jquery.min.js">
   10       </script>
   11       <script>
   12         $(document).ready(function () {
   13
   14           $('#btnDiv').click(function(){
   15             alert($('#myDiv').html()); //returns innerHtml of #myDiv
   16           });
   17
   18           //add <p>This is another paragraph.</p> to #emptyDiv
   19           $('#emptyDiv').html('<p>This is another paragraph.</p>');
   20         });
   21       </script>
   22       <style>
   23         .yellowDiv{
   24           background-color: ■yellow;
   25           margin:5px 0 0 0;
   26         }
   27       </style>
   28       </head>
   29       <body>
   30         <h1>Demo: jQuery html() method</h1>
   31         <button id="btnDiv">Get div html</button>
   32
   33         <div id="myDiv" class="yellowDiv">
   34           <p style="font-size:16px;font-weight:bold">
   35             This is paragraph.
   36           </p>
   37         </div>
   38         <div id="emptyDiv">
   39         </div>
   40       </body>
   41     </html>
```

See the screenshot below showing how you can manipulate text, styles, and attributes with jQuery using **the** jQuery text() Method.

```
contact.html ●    JS index.js    ●    # index2.css 2 ●
C > Web Design > web > <> contact.html > ⊘ html > ⊘ body
  8    <title>Simple HTML Document</title>
  9    <script src="https://ajax.googleapis.com/ajax/libs/jquery/1.11.2/jquery.min.js">
 10    </script>
 11    <script>
 12        $(document).ready(function () {
 13        $('#btnDiv').click(function(){
 14        alert($('#myDiv').text());
 15        });
 16        $('#btnP').click(function(){
 17        alert($('p').text());
 18        });
 19        //removes all the content from #emptyDiv and inserts "This is some text." to #emptyDiv
 20        $('#emptyDiv').text('This is some text.');
 21        });
 22    </script>
 23    <style>
 24    .yellowDiv{
 25        background-color:■yellow;
 26        margin:5px 0 0 0;
 27    }
 28    </style>
 29    </head>
 30    <body>
 31        <h1>Demo: jQuery text() method</h1>
 32        <button id="btnDiv">Get div text</button>
 33        <button id="btnP">Get p text</button>
 34        <div id="myDiv" class="yellowDiv">
 35            <p style="font-size:16px;font-weight:bold">
 36            This is paragraph.
 37            </p>
 38        </div>
 39        <div id="emptyDiv">
 40        </div>
 41    </body>
 42    </html>
```

Create animations and customizations with jQuery

Use the jQuery animate() function to create customized animations. The required params option defines the CSS properties that will be animated. The optional speed parameter specifies the duration of the effect. A few of the available values include "Slow," "Fast," or milliseconds. The

162

optional callback parameter is a method that is called after the animation is complete.

The example below demonstrates a simple use of the animation() method by advancing a div element to the right until it reaches the left value of 250px:

See the screenshot below showing how you can create an animation with jQuery.

```
contact.html •    JS index.js    •    # index2.css 2 •

C: > Web Design > web > ◇ contact.html > ⊘ html > ⊘ body > ⊘ p
2    <html lang="en">
3    <head>
4      <meta charset="UTF-8">
5      <meta http-equiv="X-UA-Compatible" content="IE=edge">
6      <meta name="viewport" content="width=device-width, initial-scale=1.0">
7      <link rel="stylesheet" type="text/css" rel="noopener" target="_blank" href="mystyles.css">
8      <title>Simple jQuery Document</title>
9      <script src="https://ajax.googleapis.com/ajax/libs/jquery/3.6.0/jquery.min.js"></script>
10     <script>
11     $(document).ready(function(){
12       $("button").click(function(){
13         $("div").animate({left: '250px'});
14       });
15     });
16     </script>
17     </head>
18     <body>
19       <button>Start Animation</button>
20     <p>By default, all HTML elements have a static position, and cannot be moved. To manipulate the position,
21     remember to first set the CSS position property of the element to relative, fixed, or absolute!</p>
22     <div style="background:■#98bf21;height:100px;width:100px;position:absolute;"></div>
23     </body>
24     </html>
```

Using jQuery animate() to Manipulate Multiple Properties, see screenshot below.

163

```
File  Edit  Selection  View  Go  Run  Terminal  Help                    ● contact.html - Visual Studio Code

◇ contact.html ●      JS index.js       ●     # index2.css 2  ●
C > Web Design > web > ◇ contact.html > ⊘ html > ⊘ body > ⊘ p
    2    <html lang="en">
    3    <head>
    4      <meta charset="UTF-8">
    5      <meta http-equiv="X-UA-Compatible" content="IE=edge">
    6      <meta name="viewport" content="width=device-width, initial-scale=1.0">
    7      <link rel="stylesheet" type="text/css" rel="noopener" target="_blank" href="mystyles.css">
    8      <title>Simple jQuery Document</title>
    9      <script src="https://ajax.googleapis.com/ajax/libs/jquery/3.6.0/jquery.min.js"></script>
   10      <script>
   11      $(document).ready(function(){
   12        $("button").click(function(){
   13          $("div").animate({
   14            left: '250px',
   15            opacity: '0.5',
   16            height: '150px',
   17            width: '150px'
   18          });
   19        });
   20      });
   21      </script>
   22      </head>
   23      <body>
   24        <button>Start Animation</button>
   25
   26        <p>By default, all HTML elements have a static position, and cannot be moved. To manipulate the position,
   27          remember to first set the CSS position property of the element to relative, fixed, or absolute!</p>
   28
   29        <div style="background: #08bf21;height:100px;width:100px;position:absolute;"></div>
   30      </body>
   31    </html>
```

Use your jQuery knowledge to make your website interactive

To get started with jQuery, simply add the following line to your document's <head>:

<script   src="https://code.jquery.com/jquery-2.2.3.min.js"integrity="sha256-a23g1Nt4dtEYOj7bR+vTu7+T8VP13humZFBJNIYoEJo="crossorigin="anonymous"></script>.

This will load the jQuery library from jquery.com and ensure that the given file contains the desired information. This

164

safeguards your users in the unlikely case that jquery.com is ever compromised or hacked. If a file doesn't have the expected hash signature, the browser will simply reject it and go on. Your website won't work, but no malicious code is run either.

Check to see if jQuery is working properly by opening the console in your browser. I find the Chrome console to be better. You can access it by loading your page and hitting F12 on your keyboard. Type "$('body')" into the terminal after it has opened. You must get a response with the DOM element for your website loaded. It is a clue that everything is working even though we only selected the body tag, thus nothing has changed. If you get an error message, make sure you put the code above in the document's <head>.

jQuery Selectors

Once jQuery is up and running, you can start experimenting with selectors. You can pick and choose whatever elements of your page you want to interact with or respond to using jQuery selectors. Several illustrations may be helpful:

- $('body') //: This selects the <body> tag.
- $('p') //: This selects all <p> tags throughout the document.
- $('.button') //: This selects all items with the "button" class, regardless of tag type.
- $('#aSpecificButton') //: This selects the element with the id="aSpecificButton".

To specify the items that you want jQuery to act on, you can use any arrangement of HTML tags and CSS selectors. See if you can pick out particular parts of your page by using those in the console as you practice.

jQuery Methods

So how do we go about using these selectors? Of course, we take advantage of the jQuery API. Fortunately, many of the methods with the most influence are quite simple to understand, so we won't need to tinker with the API too much to obtain the results we need. We employ conventional dot notation on our selector to call a jQuery method. Again, examples rather than explanations are more helpful in this situation:

- $('#pageTitle').html("Hello World"); // This sets the element with the id='pageTitle' to contain the text "Hello World".
- $('.error').show(); // This reveals any elements of class='error' that have been hidden.
- $('.error').hide(); // Hides all elements of class='error'.
- $('.error').toggle(); // Hides visible errors and reveals hidden ones.
- $('p').addClass('BigFont'); // Adds the class BigFont to all paragraph tags. Note that this won't do anything unless your CSS contains a definition for .BigFont.
- $('p').removeClass('BigFont'); // Removes the class BigFont from all paragraph tags.

Try experimenting with these features to see how much control you can exert over your page using just a few standard techniques. However, keep in mind that when you reload the page, everything returns to normal because your underlying HTML hasn't changed. On the client's end, all manipulation takes place.

jQuery Events

To make your page interactive, the next step is to tie these methods up to events. Thankfully, jQuery makes that rather simple as well. There are two approaches.

<button onclick="$('p').css('background-color', '#FFFF00');">Click me to make paragraphs yellow!</button>.

Or

```
<script type="text/javascript">

    $('button').click( function() { $('p').css('background-color', '#FFFF00');"> }

</script>
```

At this juncture, you can use the knowledge you have gathered so far to build your website to your taste.

Responding to user-initiated events with jQuery

Setting up event-driven replies on page components is simple with jQuery. The end user's interaction with the page, such as when text is typed into a form element or the mouse pointer is changed, frequently causes these events to occur. In some circumstances, such as the page load and unload events, the event will be started by the browser.

The majority of native browser events have convenient methods provided by jQuery. These shortcuts for jQuery.on() method include.click(),.focus(),.blur(),.change(), and others. The on method is helpful when you want to pass an object comprising many events and handlers when you want to pass data to the event handler, when you are working with custom events, or when you want to tie the same handler function to multiple events.

CHAPTER EIGHT

GIT, GITHUB, AND VERSION CONTROL

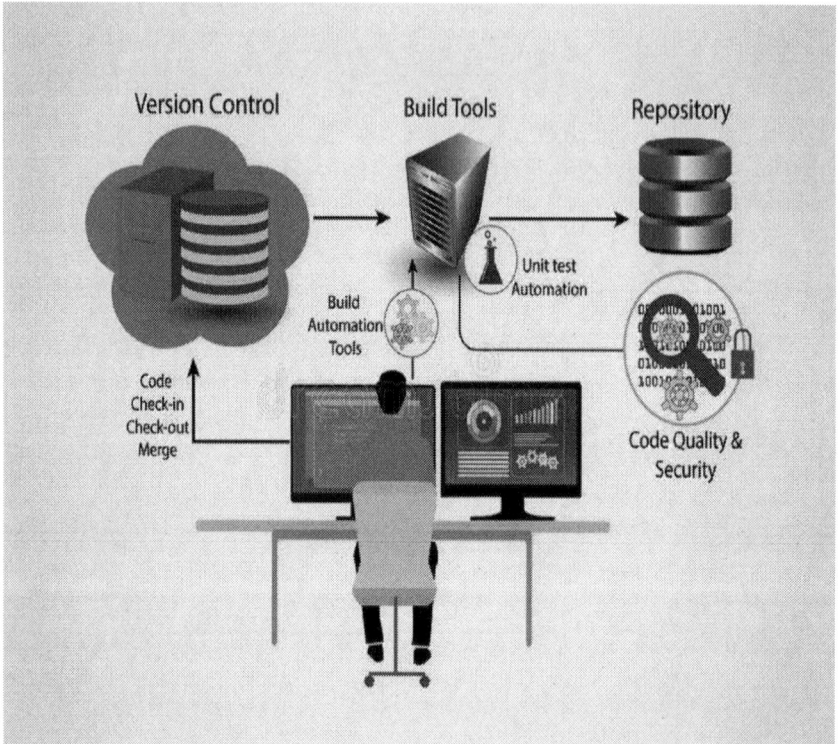

What is a version control system

To keep track, make, and manage changes to your software code, employ the use of a version control system. Additionally known as source control. Using a version control system, developers can save each modification they make to a file at various stages and later retrieve those changes with their peers.

There are three types of version control systems, which are:

- Local Version Control Systems.
- Centralized Version Control Systems.
- Distributed Version Control Systems.

What is a Local Version Control System (LVCS)?

This kind of version control system is widely used and easy to use. But because the data are being saved on your local machine, this method is very vulnerable to mistakes and attacks. As a result, you run the risk of losing the system file or forgetting the directory or folder where the file you're working is located (and then writing in another directory).

What is a Centralized Version Control System (CVCS)?

A server serves as a repository for each version of the code under this sort of version control. The CVCS facilitates developer collaboration amongst many teams. Despite the useful collaboration and communication amongst developers, there is a danger that you will lose your work if a server goes down for a short period or becomes corrupted. Unfortunately, the CVCS has a serious issue with this.

Only a small number of developers can collaborate on a project in CVCS.

What is a Distributed Version Control System (DVCS)?

The most recent and popular sort of version control system in use today is this one. In a DVCS, each developer has a complete backup (clone) of all the server's data. This means that even when the server is malfunctioning or unavailable, you can continue working on your project and restore your repositories by copying them to the server. Many developers can collaborate on a project while using a DVCS. Git is a well-known DVCS, and we'll talk more about it below.

What is Git?

Git is a distributed version control system that is open source, and free, and you may use it to track changes made to your files. Git allows you to work on all sizes of projects, from small to enormous. Git allows you to add modifications to your code and commit (or save) those changes once you're done. This implies that previous alterations can also be undone. What is GitHub since it is closely related to Git?

What is GitHub?

GitHub is a web interface where you store your Git repositories and track and manage your changes effectively. It allows different developers working on the same project access to the code. While other developers are adding modifications to a project, you can also make your own. You can quickly return to a prior stage when the issue has not yet occurred if you accidentally screw up some code in your project while making modifications.

Why use GitHub

There are so many reasons you should learn and use GitHub. Let's look at a few of them now.

1. **Effective Project Management:** Your Git repositories are stored on GitHub. Being on the same page while working on the same project from multiple locations is made simple by GitHub. You can quickly track and manage the changes you've made with GitHub, as well as keep track of how far along your project is.

2. **Simple Collaboration and Cooperation:** Using GitHub, developers from around the world may easily collaborate on a project. When working on a project together, teams can stay on the same page and manage the project efficiently.

3. **Open Source:** The GitHub platform is free and open source. This implies that developers have simple access to various kinds of code and projects that they can utilize to hone their abilities.

4. **Versatility:** GitHub's versatility quality is crucial. GitHub is not just a developer-focused web interface. Designers, authors and anyone else who wants to keep track of the progress of their projects can utilize it.

How to Setup Git

If you haven't already, you'll need to download Git to your computer before you can begin using it. By visiting their official website, you can achieve this.

Follow the procedures below:

- Open a web browser and type "https://git-scm.com" in the address bar and press enter key on the keyboard.

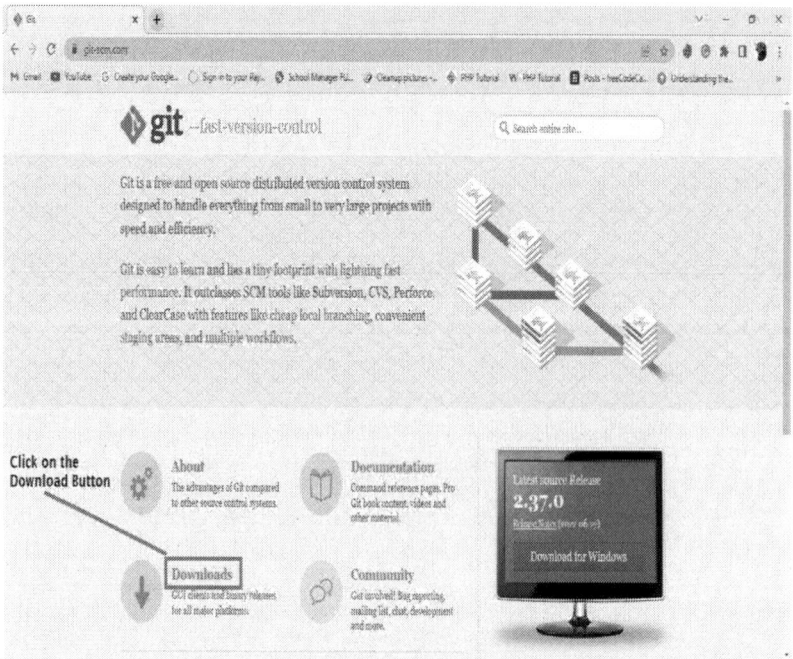

- Click on the Download button on the Git website

- Select an operating system, such as Windows, macOS, Linux, or Unix. Since I'm using a Windows machine, I'll be selecting the Windows option in my case:

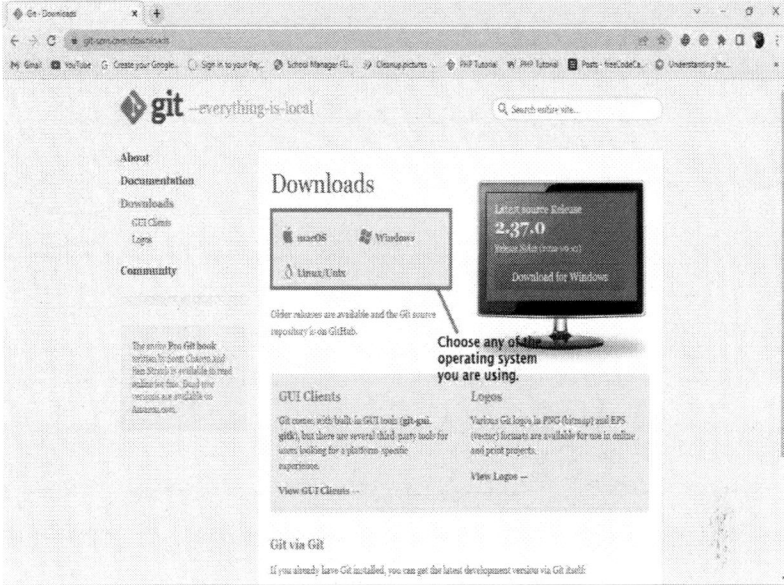

- To get the most recent version of Git, click the first link at the very top of the page. See the illustration below:

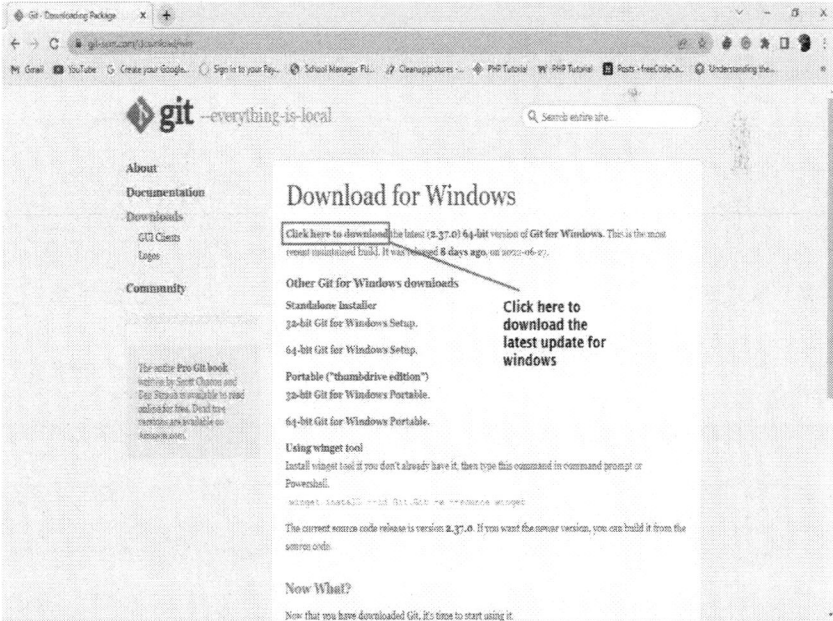

- Install Git on your computer as soon as the download is finished. You must install the file by going to the site where it was downloaded.

You should confirm that Git has been successfully installed on your machine after the installation. Run the command: git -version from the command prompt or Git bash (whichever one you like to use).

```
re@DEREK MINGW64 ~
$ git --version
git version 2.37.0.windows.1
```

Your computer should show the current version of Git beneath the command you just entered if Git was successfully installed on it. If the most recent version is shown, kudos to you!

How to Configure Git

After setting up Git on our PC, we must configure it. We do this so that we can quickly recognize the contributions we have made in the repository if we are working as a team on a project.

Using the git config —global command, we must specify the name, email address, and the branch to configure Git. For instance:

```
me@DEREK MINGW64 ~
$ git config --global user.name "Derek Emmanuel"

me@DEREK MINGW64 ~
$ git config --global user.email derekemmanuel99@gmail.com

me@DEREK MINGW64 ~
$ git config --global init.default branch main

me@DEREK MINGW64 ~
$ |
```

To set the username, we used git config —global user.name, as shown in the image above. In my situation, I went by Derek Emmanuel. The git config —global user.email has the same effect.

Git comes with a default branch named master, so I used the git config —global init.default branch main command to rename it to the main branch.

You are now ready to use Git.

How to Setup a GitHub Account

Follow the procedures below to set up your Github account:

- Visit GitHub's official website "https://github.com" to create an account. The sign-up button is located in the top right corner.

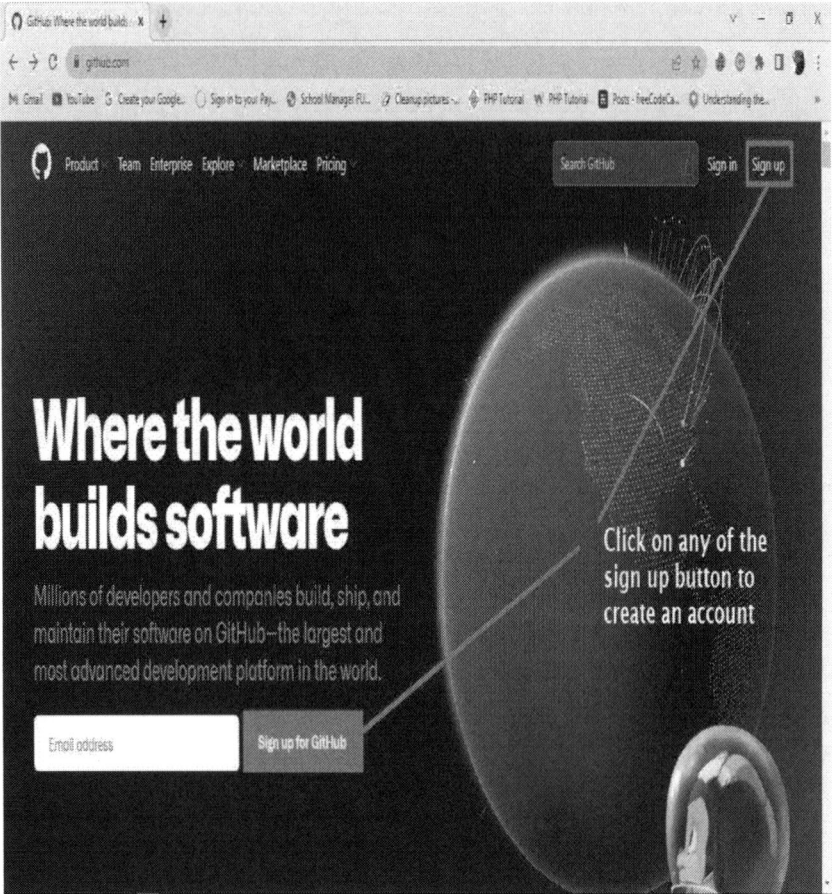

- Input your email, make a password, enter your username, and then validate your account after the signup form has opened before clicking the "new account" button.

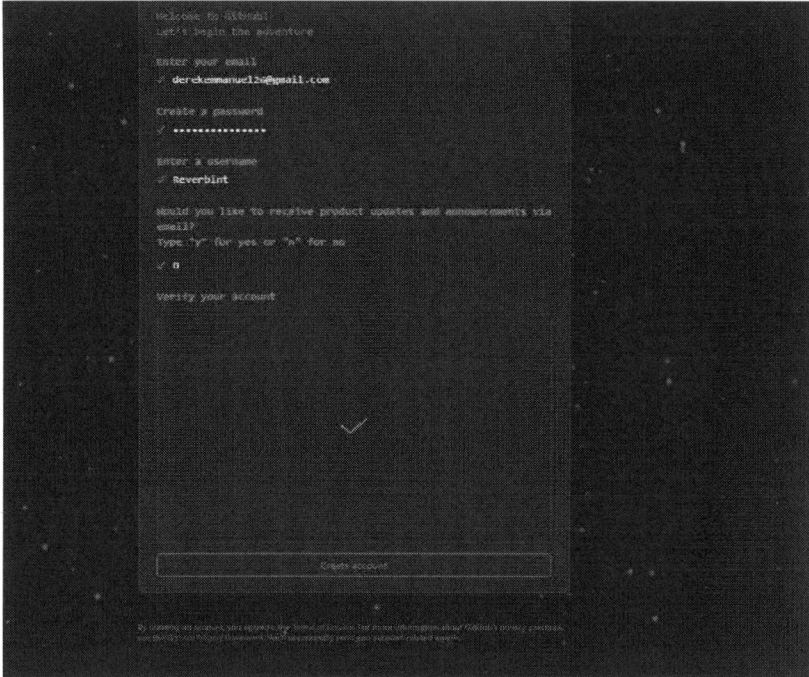

Commonly Used Git Commands

There are some basic Git commands that every developer should know how to use:

- git config
- git init
- git add
- git commit
- git clone
- git push
- git rm
- git branch

Let's go through each of these briefly so you know how to use them.

How to Use the git config Command

You can identify who made a commit when working on a project by using this command to set the username, email, and branch of a user. When you have downloaded git to your computer and wish to configure it for your needs, you run this command.

For example:

- git config --global user.name " [username]"

- git config --global user.email [email address]

How to Use the git init Command

To launch Git in your project, use the git init command. When working on a project and wishing to initialize git to the project to maintain track of the changes made in the project, use this git command.

For example:

git init

When you issue this command, you should observe an automatic creation of a .git folder in the folder you are now working in.

How to Use the git add Command

Your file gets added to the staging area with this command. The files we modify are added to the staging area, where they wait for the following commit. The git adds command is used to add a file to the staging location. The staging area receives all of the files in the folder. You can add the name of the specific file you want to commit to the staging area by using the command git add (file name). When you want to commit changes you have made to a file to your project, use this command.

How to Use the git commit Command

This commits every file in the staging area as well as any files you added with the git add command.

Use git commit-m "initial commit" as an example. This command permanently stores a file in the Git repository. When a file is added to the staging area using the git add command, you use it.

How to Use the git clone Command

A repository that already exists in another location can be copied to the present location using the git clone command.

For instance, to duplicate a Git repository from GitHub into your local storage, execute the command git clone (repository name).

How to Use the git push Command

This command is used to upload or push files from a local repository or storage to remote storage, like GitHub.

Using git push (remote storage name), for instance: Use this command only when you're ready to publish or push a project to the GitHub repository after making all the necessary changes and commits.

How to Use the git rm Command

You can remove a file from an active repository with this Git command. Take the command git rm (filename): Only remove undesired modifications or files from the Git repository by using this command.

How to Use the git branch Command

This command allows you to check the main or master branch that you are currently working on. git branch, for instance. You can use this command to find out which branch you are currently working on.

Git forking, branching, and cloning

Forking:

Forking's key benefit is that contributions can be combined without everyone having to push to a single central repository. Only the project maintainer can push to the official repository; developers push to their server-side repositories. With no write access to the official codebase, the maintainer can accept commits from any developer.

A branching approach based on the Gitflow Workflow is often followed by the forking workflow. This indicates that finished feature branches will be intended for merging into the repository of the original project maintainer. The result is a distributed workflow that offers huge, organic teams (including untrusted third parties) a customizable approach to working together safely. It is the perfect methodology for open source projects because of this.

How Forking it works

The Forking Workflow starts with an official public repository kept on a server, much like in the other Git workflows. However, a new developer does not immediately clone the official repository when they want to begin working on the project.

Instead, they make a copy of it on the server by forking the official repository. No other developers are permitted to push to this new copy, but they are permitted to pull changes from it (we'll see why this is significant in a moment). It acts as its public repository. The developer uses git clone to get a copy of their server-side copy onto their local machine after creating it. Like with the other workflows, this acts as their development environment.

They push a local commit to their public repository, not the official one when they're prepared to publish it. When an update is prepared to be incorporated, they submit a pull request to the project maintainer's main repository. If there are problems with the given code, the pull request also functions as a handy forum for discussion. A step-by-step illustration of this approach is shown below.

- An "official" server-side repository is "forked" by a developer. By doing this, they produce a server-side copy.
- Their local system is cloned with the new server-side copy.
- The local clone receives a Git remote path for the "official" repository.
- A new branch for a local feature is made.
- The new branch receives modifications from the developer.
- New commits are made for the modifications.
- The developer's server-side copy receives the branch.
- The developer opens a pull request to the 'official' repository from the new branch.
- The original server-side repository receives approval for the merge of the pull request.

The maintainer pulls the contributor's modifications into their local repository, verifies that they don't break the project, merges them into their local main branch, and then pushes the main branch to the official repository on the server to integrate the feature into the official codebase. Other developers should pull from the official repository to synchronize their local repositories now that the contribution has been accepted as part of the project.

It's crucial to realize that the Forking Workflow's use of the term "official" repository is only a convention. The fact that it is the public repository of the project maintainer is the only thing that distinguishes the official repository as being so official.

Forking vs cloning

It's crucial to remember that "forking" and "forked" repositories are not special actions. Repositories that have been forked are created using the git clone command. Repositories that have been forked are often "server-side clones" and are typically hosted and managed by a third-party Git service like Bitbucket. To establish forked repositories, there is no special Git command. A repository's history and a clone operation are essentially copies of one another.

Branching in the Forking Workflow

These personal public repositories are simply a practical mechanism for developers to exchange branches. Like with the Feature Branch Workflow and the Gitflow Workflow, everyone should continue to use branches to isolate individual features. The sharing of those branches is the only distinction. They are pushed to the official repository in the Feature Branch and Gitflow Workflows, while they are pulled into another developer's local repository in the Forking Workflow.

Fork a repository

A Forking Workflow project requires all new developers to fork the main repository. Forking is simply a typical git clone procedure, as was already mentioned. You can accomplish this by SSHing into the server and using git clone to copy the file to another location. Repo forking tools are available in well-known Git hosting platforms like Bitbucket, which automate this process.

Clone your fork

The next step is for each developer to clone their respective public forked repository. They can accomplish this using the well-known git clone tool. Developers on a project should have their Bitbucket accounts and should clone their forked copy of the repository using: Assuming Bitbucket is used to host these repositories.

For git clone use, https://user@bitbucket.org/user/repo.git.

Explore the components of back-end development, working with an MVC framework

Websites have evolved over the past few years from being straightforward HTML pages with a little CSS to very complicated programs with thousands of developers working on them concurrently. Developers put out their projects using various design patterns to deal with these sophisticated web apps, making the code simpler and easier to work with. Model View Controller, often known as MVC, is the most well-known of these patterns.

Developers can effectively manage the interaction between the user interface and underlying data by using the model-view-controller (MVC) design pattern. MVC facilitates the development of web applications by dividing the application into three logical sections. If you want to work as a web developer or in a position that is related to web development, it is beneficial to study the MVC framework. Everything you need to know about MVC frameworks, including their various parts, advantages, disadvantages, and alternatives, is covered in this article.

Model, View, and Controller are the three primary logical components that make up an application according to the Model-View-Controller (MVC) architecture, an architectural/design pattern. Each architectural element is designed to manage particular application development facets. It separates the presentation layer from the business logic layer. Historically, it was applied to desktop graphical user interfaces (GUIs). The most widely used industry standard web development framework for building scalable and flexible projects today is MVC. Mobile application design is another usage for it.

Trygve Reenskaug invented MVC. This design pattern's main objective was to address the issue of users handling a huge and complex data collection by dividing a large program into several portions, each of which had a distinct function.

attributes of MVC:

- It offers a distinct division between input logic, UI logic, and business logic.

- It provides complete control over your HTML and URLs, making the architecture of web applications simple to create.

- It is a potent URL-mapping component that allows us to create applications with understandable and searchable URLs.

- Test-Driven Development is supported (TDD).

Components of MVC:

- The MVC framework comprises the following components:

- Controller.

- Model.

View.

See the MVC Architectural Design below:

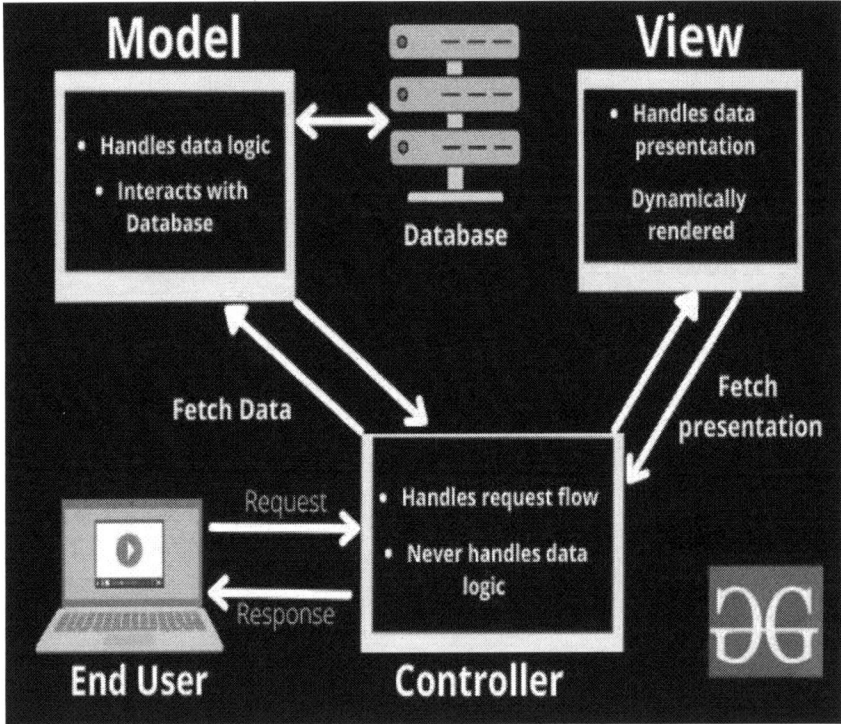

Model | Database | View

Model
- Handles data logic
- Interacts with Database

Database

View
- Handles data presentation
- Dynamically rendered

Fetch Data

Fetch presentation

Request

Controller
- Handles request flow
- Never handles data logic

Response

End User

Controller

1. Controller

The controller functions as a mediator by enabling the link between the views and the model. The controller only needs to instruct the model—it doesn't have to worry about handling data logic. To render the finished product, it processes all the business logic and incoming requests and works with the View component and the Model component to change data.

2. View

The application's entire UI functionality is implemented in the View component. For the user, it creates an interface. The data that the model component collects is what fuels views, but the data aren't taken directly; rather, they go through the controller. It only communicates to the compiler.

3. Model

All of the user's data-related logic is represented by the Model component. This could be any other data related to business logic or the data that is being passed between the View and Controller components. The database can be used to add or retrieve data. Because the controller is unable to interface with the database on its own, it answers the controller's request. The model communicates with the database and provides the controller with the necessary data.

Understand the working of the MVC framework with an example

Let's imagine an end-user sends a request to a server to get a list of students studying in a class. The server would then send that request to that particular controller that handles students. That controller would then request the model that handles students to return a list of all students studying in a class.

See the flow of Data in MVC Components in the diagram below:

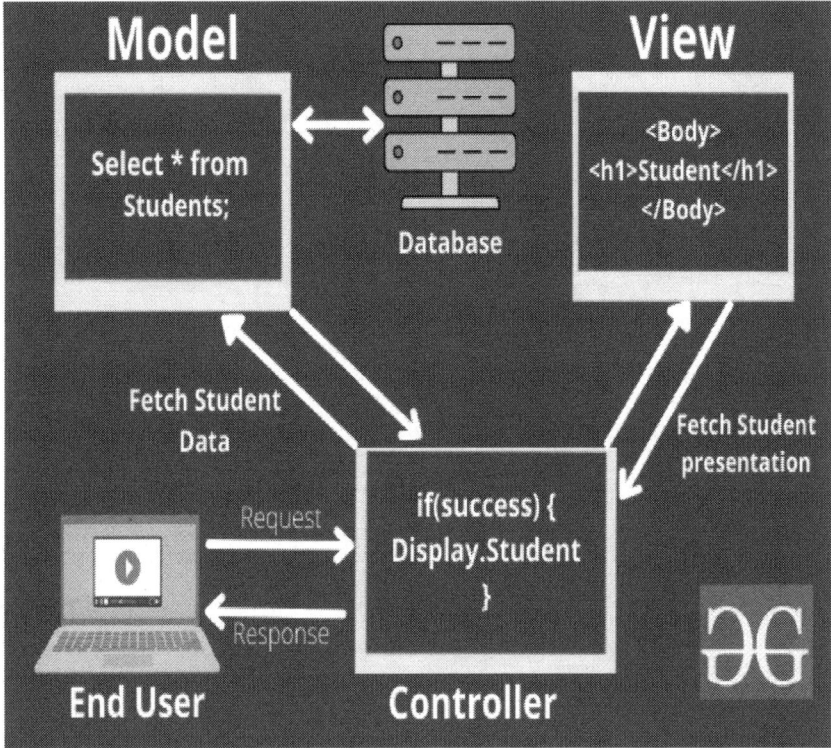

The model would ask the database to deliver a list of all students, then it would give the controller that list. The controller would ask the view related to students to return a presentation of the list of students if the answer from the model had been successful. This view would use the controller's list of students to display the list in browser-friendly HTML.

After that, the controller would take that presentation and give it to the user once more. Hence, the request is fulfilled. If the model had earlier returned an error, the controller would deal with it by instructing the view responsible for handling errors to show a presentation for that specific

190

error. The user would then receive the error presentation rather than the student list display.

The aforementioned illustration demonstrates how the model manages all of the data. The controller only instructs the model and view on what to do, while the view manages all of the presentations. The MVC framework's fundamental structure and operation are as follows.

Advantages of MVC:

- Codes are simple to maintain and may be readily expanded.
- Each element of the MVC model may be independently tested.
- MVC components can be developed concurrently.
- Separating an application into three parts lessens complexity. view, model, and controller.
- Test-Driven Development is supported (TDD).
- It functions effectively for Web applications that are backed by sizable web design and development teams.
- Because all classes and objects are independent of one another, this architecture makes it easier to test components independently.
- Supportive of search engine optimization (SEO).

Disadvantages of MVC:

- This model is challenging to read, modify, test, and reuse.
- It cannot be used to create small applications.

- A view of the inefficiencies of data access.
- Navigating the framework might be challenging since it adds new abstraction layers, forcing users to adjust to the MVC decomposition requirements.
- Increasing data inefficiency and complexity.

Popular MVC Frameworks

The following list includes some of the most well-known and widely used MVC frameworks.

- Ruby on Rails.
- Django.
- CherryPy.
- Spring MVC.
- Catalyst.
- Rails.
- Zend Framework.
- Fuel PHP.
- Laravel.
- Symphony.

(NB: Applications that run on a single graphical workstation typically employ MVC. The separation of logical components improves readability and modularity while also making the testing portion more comfortable).

How to use Github with Xcode

A selection of tools from Xcode can help you streamline your GitHub flow. Let's go over a few GitHub integrations with Xcode.

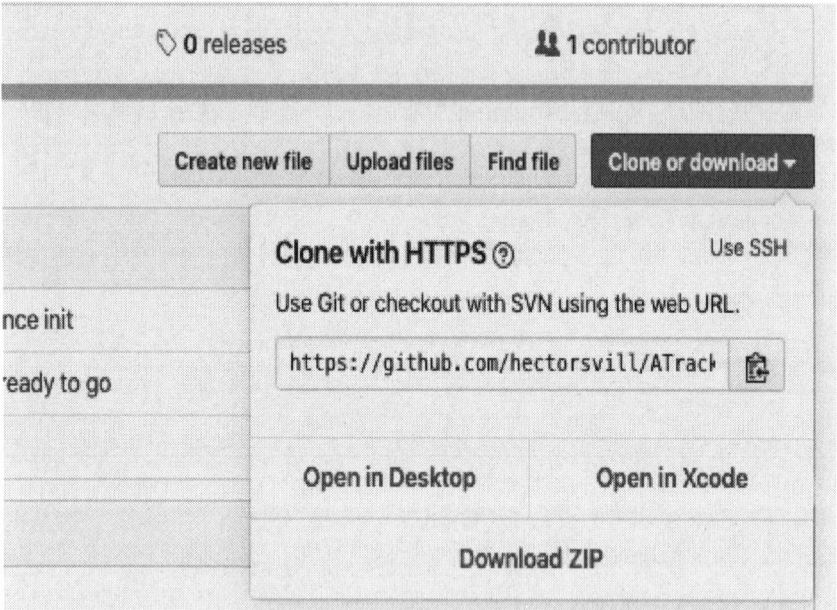

There are a few preliminary steps we need to complete on our Mac (if you're using Xcode, I'm assuming you're on a Mac) before we can guarantee Github is configured properly. So, before we start, there are three things we need to accomplish. We must open a terminal to get things started. Second, we need to make changes to the ".gitconfig" file in our Home directory. Third, we need to log into our Github account using Xcode! Let's move forward!

- First, Let's begin by launching the terminal. To open the spotlight search, press "command + space," type "terminal," and hit enter. There will be a terminal!
- Second, let's begin configuring our Github user name and email in the terminal. To check and configure your credentials, use the "git config" command. Keep in mind that your commits will be linked to this email address. "Mona Lisa" is entered in the global user.name and global user.email fields of the git configuration command.
- Third, we must use Xcode to sign into our Github account. So let's use Spotlight Search to launch Xcode. To enter Xcode, hit "command +, " once there. Now the Preference window ought to appear. Go to "Accounts" and click the "+" icon in the bottom left corner to log in to your Github account from Xcode. You can enter your Github username and password after selecting Github and pressing confirm.

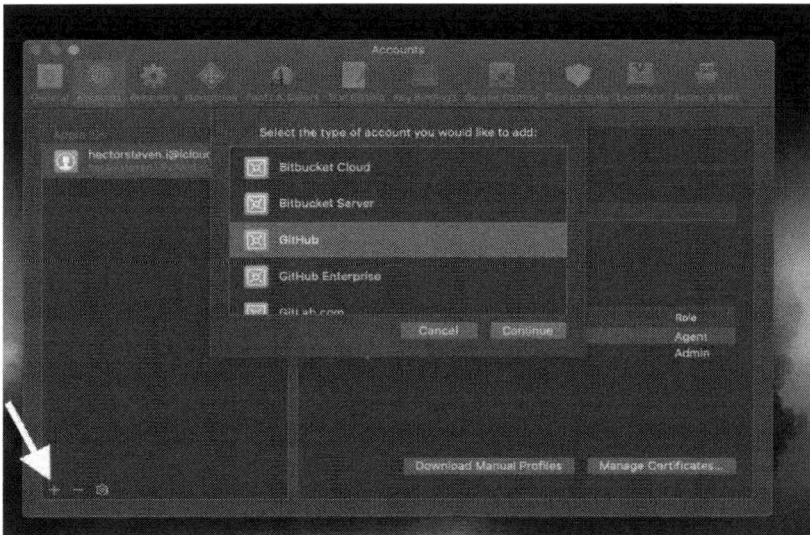

Create a repository on Github with Xcode

You don't need to leave Xcode, as I previously stated. First, directly from Xcode, let's build a Github repository! This is the approach I prefer! Second, after creating the repository on Github, we'll show you how to add a remote to your Xcode project.

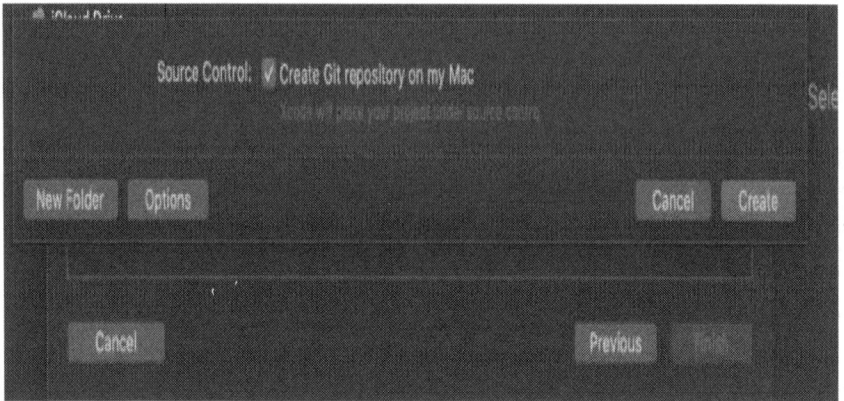

You may create a Git repository on your Mac when you start an Xcode project for the first time. However, you may also complete this step after starting your project by heading to your bar items, selecting "Source Control," and then selecting "Create Git Repositories..." As you can see, we may also commit, push, pull, and reject any modifications from this point.

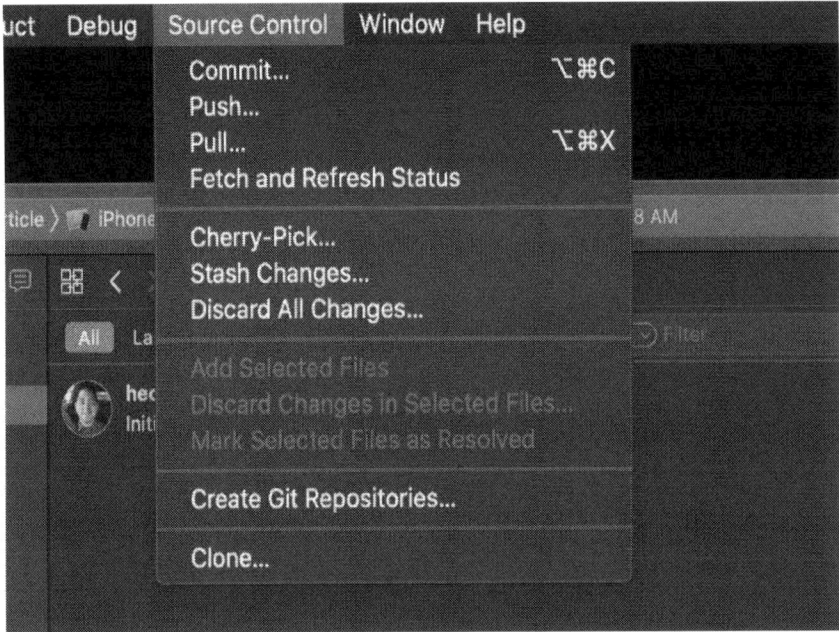

By pressing "command + 2," we can now display the Source Control Navigator. There are a few folders when you open the folder structure. Remotes are the ones we're looking for. Using Control + Click, choose the folder, then select Create "Your Project" Remote...

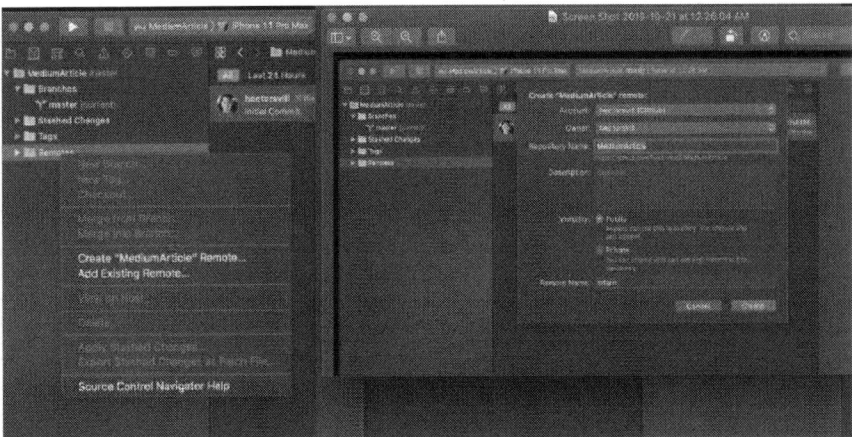

A new window will open, allowing you to name and describe the repository, as well as choose whether to make it public or private. When you open Github.com after pressing create, the newly formed repository will be listed under Repositories.

Adding an existing remote

Once the Github repository has been created, this can also be done. All you would have to do is take the current remote.

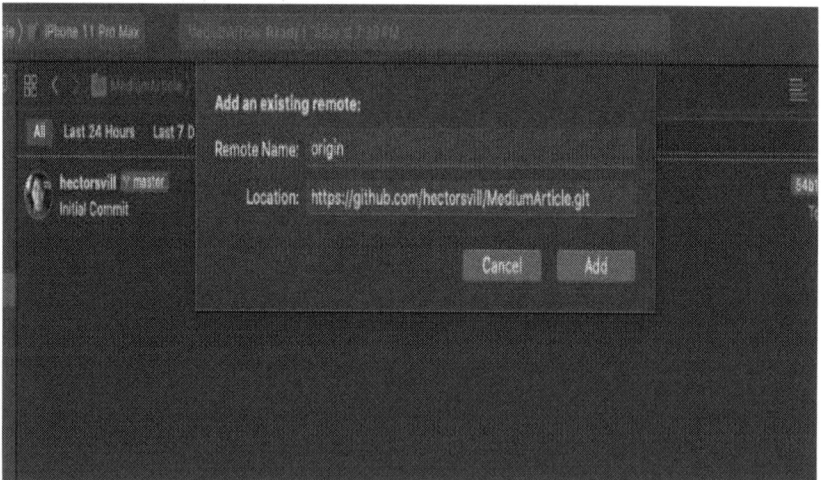

Control + click on Remotes in the Source Control Navigator, then select Add Existing Remote. It will open a window where you can enter the remote name and location. However, the Location must be set to your git remote. You can leave Remote Name as an origin. Make certain that your Location ends in .git!

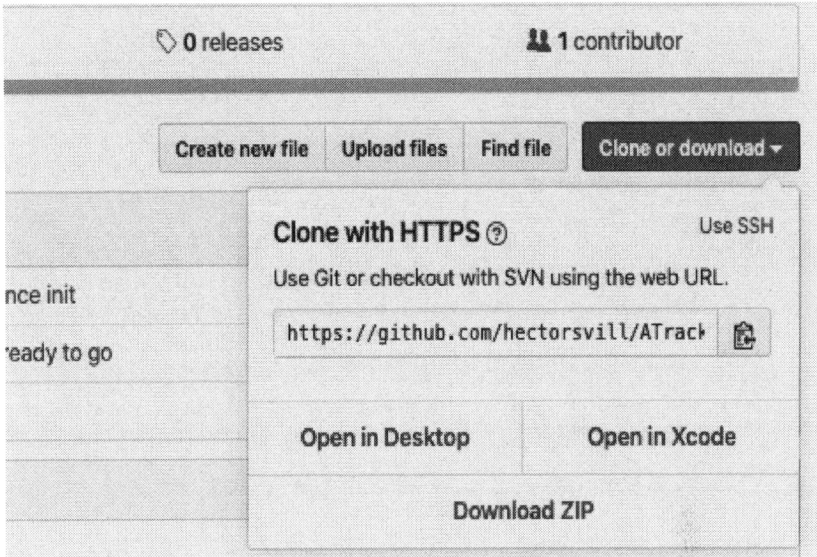

You may now find the project with an "Open in Xcode" button if you click on the Clone or Download button.

Branching with Xcode

Branch creation is possible through the Source Control Navigator.

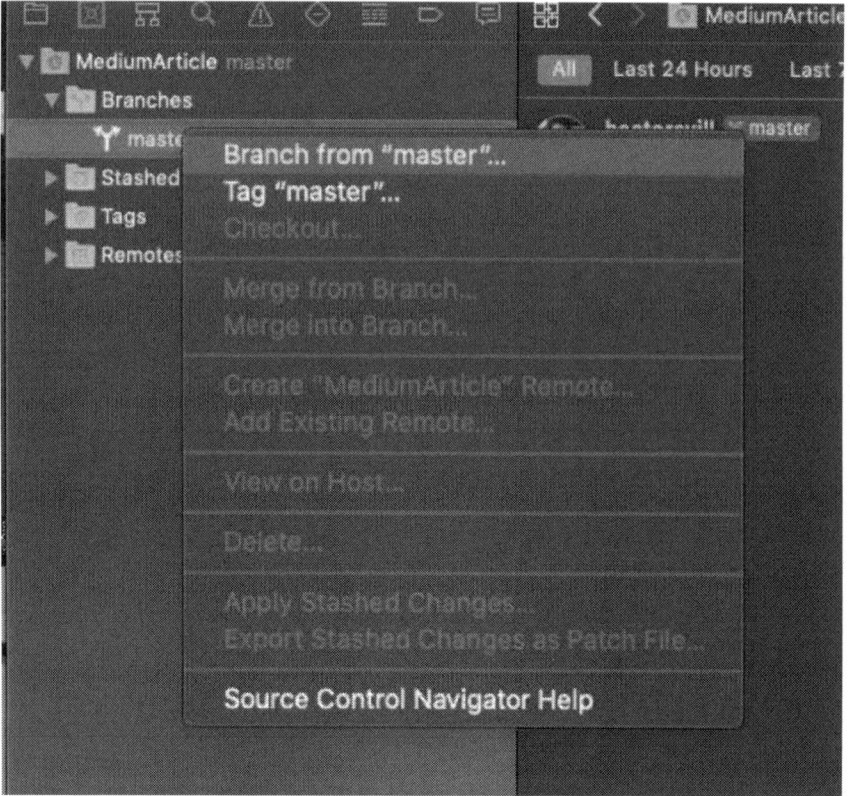

You can always use "cmd + 2" to navigate around this site. To begin, control + click the branch you want to leave. You'll now be shown a window where you can give that branch a name. The newly created branch will appear in the Branches folder.

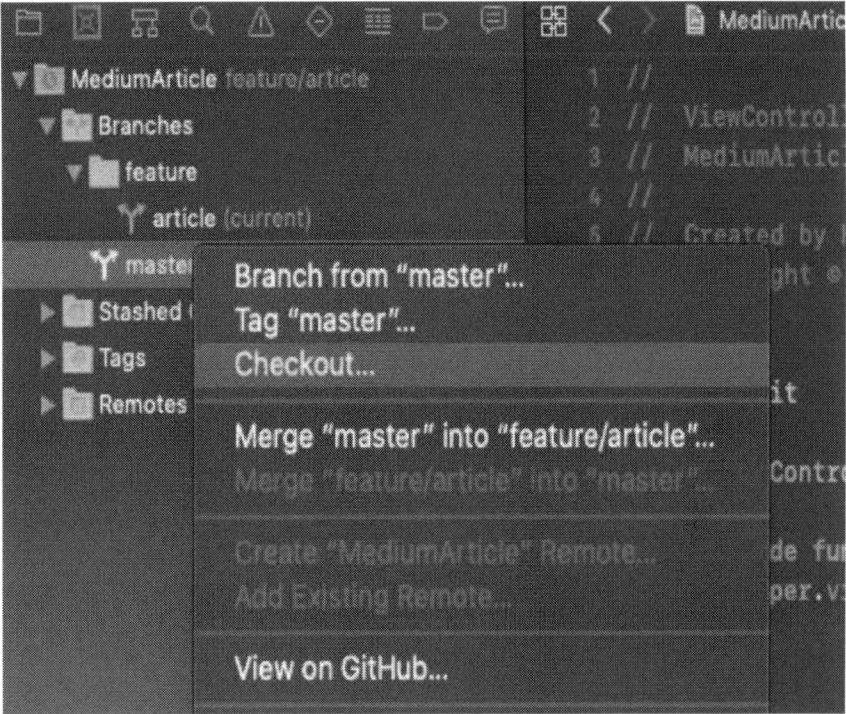

By using Control + Clicking on the branch and pressing Checkout, you can quickly check out from it. You will now be on the chosen branch as a result of this.

Committing to Github with Xcode

"Option + Command + C" is the shortcut for committing in Xcode. The window you see below will appear as a result.

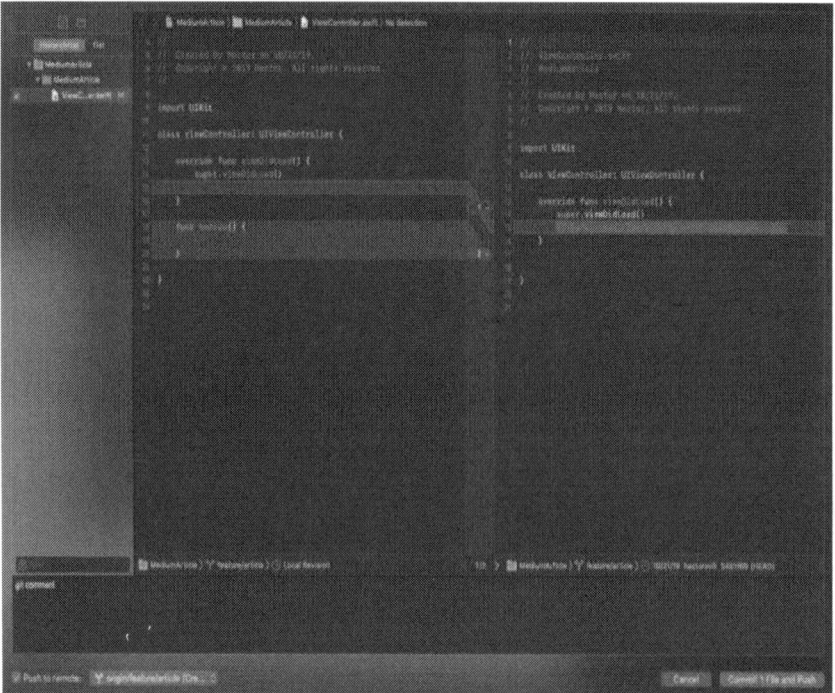

This robust tool for tracking your commits will highlight three key aspects. You may first view every modified file on the Navigator. You can choose whatever files you want to commit here. You may also examine the precise modifications that were made to that file. Third, you can push the changes to a particular branch using the Push to Remote option located in the bottom left corner.

CONCLUSION

Developers can keep up with the rapid changes in technology since full-stack development requires a wide variety of abilities. They can construct the full working prototype on their own because they are familiar with every layer of the technology stack. Organizations that need to create a Minimum Feasible Product as quickly as possible while considering the needs of the client will benefit from the capacity of full stack developers to operate across various stacks.

Every full stack developer should be able to work on every layer of the application and produce finished products in the shortest amount of time. The market need for full-stack web developers has grown as a result of their contribution to many stages of the development life cycle. You must understand all the skills you require if you want to work as a full-stack developer.

This publication is put up for you to straighten the crooked paths on your journey to becoming a full-stack Web Developer, revealing to you what you need to know. That is, knowing what you need in this career journey to make the journey sweet and easygoing.

This publication series is focused on the modern Front-end development technologies and the next series shall discuss the Back-end technology tools alongside the Database technology tools and every other technology involved in the modern-day full-stack development tools.

INDEX

DVCS, 36
dynamic, 162

Form, 53, 54
FOSS, 158
frame, 113
framework, 18, 81, 100, 166, 195, 196, 197, 198, 200, 201
frameworks, 13, 17, 28, 30, 31, 81, 196, 201
front end, 13, 14, 28, 29, 30, 31, 166
frontend, 28, 29, 30
front-end, 12, 14, 18, 19
front-end, 30
front-end, 33
front-end, 100
front-end, 166
Frontend, 28
FTP, 24
full stack, 12, 15, 16, 17, 18, 211
Full Stack, 12, 13, 14, 16, 29
full-stack, 15, 16, 17, 18, 19, 20, 21, 22, 29, 211
function, 111, 122, 132, 145, 162, 164, 167
functionalities, 27, 116, 147
functions, 29, 132, 139, 140, 145, 153, 165, 192
Functions, 131, 147

G

games, 12, 27
gedit, 51
generic, 98
Geolocation, 54
getElementById, 152
git, 190, 207
Git, 35, 36, 40, 181, 183, 184, 185, 186, 189, 190, 194, 205
Github, 203, 204, 206
GitHub, 20, 31, 35, 36, 38, 40, 181, 182, 186, 187, 190, 191, 202
global, 122, 203
Global, 122
GNU, 41
Google, 23, 33, 46, 107, 166
graphic, 27, 42, 102, 104
graphical, 40, 102
Grid, 101, 109
guidelines, 66

H

handlers, 160
head, 56, 66, 112, 118
header, 70, 72
headers, 114
headings, 50

height, 93
Helvetica, 90
Heroku, 20
hierarchical, 140
hierarchy, 84, 106, 152
homepage, 70
hosting, 40
href, 62, 156
html, 67
HTML, 13, 14, 18, 20, 27,
    28, 29, 30, 31, 33, 35, 48,
    49, 50, 51, 53, 54, 55, 56,
    57, 58, 59, 60, 61, 62, 63,
    66, 67, 68, 69, 70, 71, 72,
    73, 74, 75, 76, 77, 78, 79,
    80, 81, 83, 86, 87, 88, 100,
    101, 109, 112, 117, 118,
    134, 149, 150, 151, 152,
    155, 156, 158, 159, 160,
    161, 162, 168, 170, 176,
    177, 195, 196, 200
HTML5, 18, 25, 30, 49, 59,
    66, 68
HTTP, 18, 20
Https, 23
Hyper, 48
hyperlinks, 50, 62
Hyperlinks, 62

I

icons, 104
id, 155
ID, 86, 87, 98, 99, 156
identified, 87
Identifiers, 85
IDEs, 117
IEEE, 41, 126
Iframes, 53
IIS, 32
image, 62, 67, 110
images, 23, 33, 50, 51, 53,
    62, 67
Images, 62, 101
implement, 72
inherit, 143
Inherit, 94
inheritance, 112, 138, 140
Inheritance, 140
inherited, 81
initial, 58
inline, 67, 112
Inline, 53
input, 68, 110, 121
Input, 54
install, 52, 160, 185
Install, 185
installation, 185
installed, 51, 185

Q

72, 77, 79, 81, 88, 100,
101, 103, 105, 106, 109,
110, 114, 115, 160, 174,
175, 177, 183, 187

Website, 60

websites, 12, 23, 24, 25, 27,
33, 53, 66, 68, 77, 92, 93,
100, 101, 104, 113, 149,
158, 160, 162, 166

Websites, 195

Wide, 51

width, 57

window, 206, 208

Windows, 42, 52

wireframe, 104

wireframes, 103

WordPress, 27, 28, 100

worldwide, 34

wrapped, 140

WWW, 22

X

Xcode, 202, 203, 204, 205, 209

XPath, 99

Z

zoom, 58

Printed in Poland
by Amazon Fulfillment
Poland Sp. z o.o., Wrocław
23 September 2022

c2b19d93-6a0d-46dd-8d42-ad231929102eR02